Irwin Grammar Skills

Robert J. Ireland

Irwin Publishing
Toronto/Vancouver, Canada

Copyright © 2002 by Irwin Publishing Ltd.

National Library of Canada Cataloguing in Publication Data

Ireland, Robert J., 1936-
    Irwin grammar skills

ISBN 0-7725-2919-1

1. English language—Grammar. I. Title.

PE 1112.I728 2002   428.2   C2001-901194-6

    This book is protected by copyright. No part of it may be reproduced or transmitted in any form or by any means, electronic or mechanical, including photocopy, recording, or any information storage and retrieval system now known or to be invented, without the prior written permission of the publisher, except by a reviewer who wishes to quote brief passages in connection with a review written for inclusion in a magazine, newspaper, or broadcast.

    Any request for photocopying, recording, taping, or for storing of informational and retrieval systems, of any part of this book should be directed in writing to CANCOPY (Canadian Reprography Collective), One Yonge Street, Suite 1900, Toronto, ON M5E 1E5

Editor: Shirley Tessier
Copy Editor: Lina Mockus-O'Brien

Published by
Irwin Publishing Limited
325 Humber College Blvd.
Toronto, Ontario
M9W 7C3

Printed and bound in Canada
1 2 3 4   05 04 03 02 01

The author and publisher would like to thank the following reviewers for their valuable insights and suggestions.
Alan Cockell, Simcoe County School Board
Gail Ebbisen, Durham District School Board
Henry Knoop, Durham District School Board
Heather Murray, Kawartha, Pine Ridge District School Board

We acknowledge for their financial support of our publishing program the Canada Council, the Ontario Arts Council, and the Government of Canada through the Book Publishing Industry Development Program (BPIDP).

Contents

Introduction:
HOW THIS BOOK IS ORGANIZED 1

Part One:
THE PARTS OF SPEECH 3
   How to Identify Nouns 4
   The Plurals of Nouns 6
   The Possessives of Nouns 8
   Review: Using Nouns 11
   Personal Pronouns 13
   Possessive Pronouns 14
   Pronouns and Antecedents 16
   Demonstrative and Interrogative Pronouns 17
   Indefinite Pronouns 19
   Pronouns and Noun Markers 21
   Review: Using Pronouns 22
   How to Identify Verbs 24
   The Parts of a Verb 27
   Verb Tenses 28
   The Principal Parts of a Verb 30
   Linking Verbs 31
   Contractions and Possessive Pronouns 32
   Irregular Verbs (1) 33
   Irregular Verbs (2) 35
   Irregular Verbs (3) 36
   Review: Using Verbs 38
   Using Adjectives 39
   Adjectives in Comparisons 40
   Using Adverbs 42
   Adverbs in Comparisons 44
   Adjective or Adverb? 45
   Adjectives and Adverbs to Note 47
   Review: Using Modifiers 49
   Prepositions 50
   Prepositional Phrases as Modifiers 52
   Preposition or Adverb? 54
   Conjunctions 55

Review: Using Prepositions and Conjunctions 56
The Parts of Speech 58
Words Used in Different Ways 60
Review: The Parts of Speech 61

Part Two:

THE SENTENCE 65
Simple Subjects and Predicates 66
Finding the Subject and the Predicate 67
Agreement in Number 69
Agreements to Watch For 70
Review: Making Subjects and Verbs Agree 71
When the Subject Doesn't Come First 72
Nouns Used as Subjects 74
Pronouns Used as Subjects 76
Direct Objects 77
Indirect Objects 78
Review: How Nouns Are Used in Sentences 79
Object Form of Pronouns 81
Transitive and Intransitive Verbs 82
Subjective Completions 83
Predicate Nouns 85
Predicated Adjectives 86
Direct Object or Subjective Completion? 88
Pronouns as Subjective Completions 89
Compound Parts in a Sentence 92
Review: The Sentence and Its Parts 93
Kinds of Sentences 95
Sentence Fragments 96
Review: Using Complete Sentences 98
Compound Constructions 100
Compound Subjects and Verb Agreements 102
Simple Sentences 103
Compound Sentences 104
Punctuating Compound Sentences 107
The Subordinate Clause 109
The Complex Sentence 112
Noun Clauses 113
Adverb Clauses 115
Adjective Clauses 117
Review: Subordinate Clauses 119
Variety in Sentence Beginnings 121
Compound–Complex Sentences 123
Review: Using Compound and Complex Sentences 125
The Last Word 127

INTRODUCTION

How this book is organized

You already know a great deal of grammar. If you did not know something about English grammar, you would be unable to speak so that others can understand you, you would not understand what people say to you, and you would be unable to read or write. However, you may not know how to talk about the grammar that you know. The purpose of this book is to help you learn to identify the parts of speech and how those parts of speech are combined to make sentences. If you can identify and name the parts of speech and the parts of a sentence, you will be able to discuss written language to see how writers use language and how you can improve your own writing. Knowing the names of English grammar structures may also help you learn another language.

The book is divided into two parts. Part One is on the parts of speech. These are the building blocks of sentences. In Part Two, we examine sentences. How are the parts of speech used in sentences? In what forms do these words appear? What kinds of sentences are there?

In a companion book, *Irwin Writing Skills*, we look at sentences from the point of view of style and effectiveness. In this book, we look at sentences from the perspective of structure and correctness.

This book contains many suggestions for applying grammar to writing. These are enclosed in boxes. We urge you to make use of these applications because, while identifying the parts of speech is an important skill, it is only of use if you can apply it to becoming a better writer. For example, an employer is not likely to ask you to identify predicate adjectives, but *will* expect you to express yourself effectively and clearly.

These are the major purposes of this book:

- To make you aware of the grammar that you already know
- To help you identify the parts of speech and how they are used in sentences
- To help you write sentences using different kinds of structures
- To help you write sentences to achieve various purposes
- To give you a vocabulary to discuss writing so that you can write correctly and effectively
- To give you an understanding of the rules of the correct mechanics of writing

When you have worked through this book, you will be better able to use your knowledge of grammar to proofread your written work.

IRWIN GRAMMAR SKILLS

PART ONE

The Parts of Speech

How to Identify Nouns 4	Adjective or Adverb? 45
The Plurals of Nouns 6	Adjectives and Adverbs to Note 47
The Possessives of Nouns 8	Review: Using Modifiers 49
Review: Using Nouns 11	Prepositions 50
Personal Pronouns 13	Prepositional Phrases as Modifiers ..52
Possessive Pronouns 14	Preposition or Adverb? 54
Pronouns and Antecedents 16	Conjunctions 55
Demonstrative and Interrogative Pronouns 17	Review: Using Prepositions and Conjunctions 56
Indefinite Pronouns 19	The Parts of Speech 58
Pronouns and Noun Markers 21	Words Used in Different Ways 60
Review: Using Pronouns 22	Review: The Parts of Speech 61
How to Identify Verbs 24	
The Parts of a Verb 27	
Verb Tenses 28	
The Principal Parts of a Verb 30	
Linking Verbs.....................31	
Contractions and Possessive Pronouns 32	
Irregular Verbs (1) 33	
Irregular Verbs (2) 35	
Irregular Verbs (3) 36	
Review: Using Verbs 38	
Using Adjectives 39	
Adjectives in Comparisons 40	
Using Adverbs 42	
Adverbs in Comparisons 44	

IRWIN GRAMMAR SKILLS

HOW TO IDENTIFY NOUNS

You know how to use nouns. However, you may not be able to identify nouns when you see them. Nouns are one of the two building blocks of sentences. It will help to be able to identify nouns so that you use them correctly in the sentences you write. **A noun often names a person, place, or thing.**

Nouns are easy to find because most of them have markers or signs. The most common signs are:

Articles	Possessive pronouns	Indefinite pronouns	Demonstrative pronouns
a	my	some	this
an	your	any	that
the	his	many	these
	her	each	those
	its	every	
	our		
	their		

You will learn more about pronouns later. For now, just think of these words as noun markers. They show that a noun is coming.

Sometimes another word or group of words comes between the marker and the noun it marks. Sometimes nouns do not have markers.

Another clue to nouns is that some of them refer to things that can be counted; that is, they may be singular or plural.
Examples:
    desk/desks   movie/movies   church/churches

Most nouns are **common nouns**, the ones you use every day and which refer to common things or ideas. Some nouns refer to a specific person or place. To show the meaning refers to a certain person or place, these nouns are capitalized. They are called **proper nouns**.
Example:
    My uncle lives in the white house.
    My uncle lives in the White House.

In the first sentence, the reference is to the house that is white. In the second sentence, the capital letters show that we mean one specific white house—the residence of the President of the United States. Did you notice another noun marker in each sentence? The word "my" marks the noun "uncle."
Some other examples:

Common Nouns	Proper Nouns
team	Edmonton Oilers
author	Margaret Atwood
university	Simon Fraser University

Part One: The Parts of Speech

To summarize, here are four ways to identify nouns:
1) nouns often refer to a person, place, or thing
2) nouns often follow an article or other noun marker
3) nouns change form as the meaning changes from singular to plural
4) nouns may be common or proper

Identify nouns

Underline all the nouns in the following sentences. Use the clues suggested above to find them. Indicate whether a noun is common or proper.

1. Some writers become very famous. _____

2. Reporters often use their experiences in the books they write. _____

3. *The National Post* was established in the year 1998. _____

4. Many small communities publish a newspaper. _____

5. Many colleges offer courses to help students learn to write well. _____

6. The study of journalism prepares a person to work for newspapers or magazines. _____

7. In Canada, it is hard for a writer to become famous. _____

8. Books from the United States dominate the shelves in stores in Canada. _____

9. Stephen King sells many books in this country. _____

10. The men and women who write the articles in magazines enjoy their work. _____

11. *Maclean's* is the largest selling magazine in Canada. _____

12. The process of writing is a challenge. _____

13. Writers need skills in the different forms of writing. _____

14. The people they meet, the places they go, are the basis for their stories. _____

15. A writer needs the content to be interesting and
    the grammar to be correct.   _____

16. Writers also need the determination to get better
    and better.   _____

There are 49 nouns in the sentences above. Did you find them all?

> Look over some of your recent writing in any subject. Find the nouns that you have used. Notice the noun markers. Notice the proper nouns. Sometimes writers forget to capitalize proper nouns. Have you missed any lately?

THE PLURALS OF NOUNS

You have learned that nouns are one of the building blocks of a sentence. Because nouns are so important, you need to be able to identify them easily.

To form the plurals of most nouns, just add "s":
    table/tables   plan/plans   chart/charts

When the singular noun ends in "s," "sh," "ch," "x," or "z," add "es":
    dress/dresses   bush/bushes
    box/boxes   church/churches

For most singular nouns that end in "o," add "s":
    photo/photos   auto/autos   stereo/stereos

For a few nouns that end in "o," add "es":
    hero/heroes   echo/echoes
    tomato/tomatoes   potato/potatoes

When a singular noun ends in "y" with a consonant before the "y," change the "y" to "i" and add "es":
    story/stories   copy/copies   dairy/dairies

When a singular noun ends in "y" with a vowel before the "y," just add "s":
    toy/toys   journey/journeys

For some singular nouns ending in "f," add "s." For many others ending in "f" or "fe," change the "f" to "v" and add "es":
    roof/roofs   chief/chiefs   wife/wives
    thief/thieves   shelf/shelves

PART ONE: THE PARTS OF SPEECH

Some nouns have the same form for both singular and plural:
    sheep/sheep   salmon/salmon   trout/trout

The plurals of some nouns are quite unusual:
    tooth/teeth   woman/women   child/children

You might be wondering why there are so many ways to form plurals. The answer lies in the long history of the English language. Some words in our language have French origins, many others came from Germanic languages, others are from Latin, etc. Language changes constantly, so there are no simple rules that apply to all words. You might be surprised to learn that the best way to learn all these different spellings is to read a lot.

Important note: *Plurals never contain an apostrophe.* If you see a plural noun written with an apostrophe, it is wrong. No matter where you might read it or who might have written it, if the plural contains an apostrophe, it is wrong. (Sorry if we got a little worked up over that. It is an error that is becoming more and more common. It is still an error no matter how often you see it.)

When you study the possessives of nouns, you will see that plural possessives may contain an apostrophe (e.g., the students' common room). However, plural possessives are not used as nouns. They are used as adjectives or noun markers. You will learn about possessives in the next exercise.

FORM THE PLURALS

Write the plural form of each of the following nouns.

1. party   _____
2. alley   _____
3. radio _____
4. dish _____
5. fox _____
6. potato _____
7. foot _____
8. man _____
9. deer _____
10. porch _____
11. solo _____
12. scarf _____

13. minute   _____

14. piano   _____

15. day   _____

16. baby   _____

If you are in doubt about a plural form, look up the word in a dictionary. There you will find both the singular and the plural spellings.

> Check over some of your recent written work. Have you been making spelling mistakes with the plural forms of words? If you have, find the plurals you have misspelled and write the correct spellings.

THE POSSESSIVES OF NOUNS

You have learned that nouns change in form to show the plural. We emphasized that when we write the plural of nouns, we never use an apostrophe. Now you will learn when you *do* use an apostrophe.

Look at the sentences below and note the use of the apostrophe.
Mel revved the engine of the car.
Mel revved the car's engine.

The winning touchdown was scored in the final minute of the game.
The winning touchdown was scored in the game's final minute.

How does the use of the apostrophe change the sentence? What words does the apostrophe replace? In these sentences, an apostrophe was used to show that something was part of something else (the engine is part of the car; the minute is part of the game).

Here are some different examples.
That coat belongs to Pat.
That is Pat's coat.

That station wagon is owned by the principal.
That is the principal's station wagon.

How is the apostrophe used in these sentences? Here the apostrophe is used to show that something (or someone) possesses or owns something. (Pat owns the coat; the station wagon belongs to the principal.)

Nouns may be adapted to show ownership or possession; that is, that one thing belongs to another, or that it is part of another thing. That may sound complicated, but you use possessive nouns every day.

PART ONE: THE PARTS OF SPEECH

In speaking, the words "cars" and "car's" sound the same. The rest of the conversation, or the **context**, shows whether we are talking about more than one car or just about the ownership of one car. In writing, we use an apostrophe to show the difference. Notice again that an apostrophe always shows ownership or possession. An apostrophe never shows the plural.

There is a simple rule for showing the possessive. If the noun you are making possessive ends in any letter other than "s," add an apostrophe and "s" ('s). If the noun ends in "s," just add an apostrophe. Here is the same rule in detail.
If the noun is singular, add an apostrophe and "s" ('s):
    player/player's glove   cook/cook's spoon
If the noun is plural and ends in "s," just add the apostrophe:
    students/students' lockers   girls/girls' change room
If the noun is plural but does not end in "s," add an apostrophe and "s" ('s):
    children/children's books   geese/geese's wings.
These rules for formation apply to both common and proper nouns.

FORM THE POSSESSIVES

Write the possessive form of each of the following nouns.

1. city   _____
2. cities   _____
3. cousin   _____
4. runners   _____
5. county   _____
6. boys   _____
7. people   _____
8. lawyers   _____
9. worker   _____
10. week   _____
11. men   _____
12. mouse   _____
13. mice   _____
14. driver   _____
15. Kathy   _____

Notice that when a noun is made possessive, it tells us something about another noun that follows it. Look back at the examples above. You will see that the possessive noun is placed before another noun and it tells something about that second noun. A possessive noun is another kind of noun marker. It will always be followed by a noun (although other words may come between them). Once in a while a possessive noun comes after the noun it describes, but we will not work with those in this exercise.

Form the possessives. Write the possessive form of each italicized word.

1. Tim enjoyed the *dancers* performance. _____
2. *Mr. Robinson* house is for sale. _____
3. The *doctor* examination was complete. _____
4. The *group* campsite was in a swamp. _____
5. The class studied the *province* history. _____
6. Everyone liked *Giselle* idea. _____
7. The *runners* faces showed the strain. _____
8. The exterminator put a cage outside the *mice* hole. _____
9. The engineer checked the *train* speed. _____
10. The *company* records have been examined. _____

In your reading, writing or conversation you might find possessive nouns that are not marked with an apostrophe. For example, "group leader," "company picnic," "school assembly." These are correct uses, but we have used only marked possessives in these exercises.

PART ONE: THE PARTS OF SPEECH

REVIEW: USING NOUNS

You now have several ways to identify nouns:
- nouns show number; a noun may be singular or plural
- nouns often follow markers such as
    articles: a, an, the, some
    possessive pronouns: my, your, his, her, our, their
    possessive nouns: farm's, Toni's, schools'
- nouns may be common or proper: woman, Queen Elizabeth
- nouns often signify a person, place, or thing

Use all these methods for identifying nouns in the following review exercises.

RECOGNIZE NOUNS

Circle each noun in the following sentences. Underline any noun markers that appear.

1. Summer is my favourite season.
2. Randy got a job to make some extra money.
3. My friends go to parties at Lakeland Beach.
4. Camping trips and hikes are a great form of exercise.
5. The girls' swimming team won the provincial championship.

(There are 15 nouns and 7 noun markers.)

FORM THE PLURAL

Write the plural form of each of the following nouns.

1. leaf
2. foot
3. block
4. potato
5. stereo
6. deer
7. fortress
8. wasp
9. county
10. buyer

FORM THE POSSESSIVES

Write the possessive form of each italicized word.

1. The team checked the *car* tires. _____
2. The *mechanic* opinion was ignored. _____
3. The previous *day* rain made the track slippery. _____
4. The managers were influenced by the *crowd* booing. _____
5. The *drivers* skills would be tested. _____

PLURAL VS. POSSESSIVE

If the italicized noun is plural, write "plural." If the noun is a possessive noun, write it with the correct spelling and the use of an apostrophe if needed.

1. The changing *seasons* give us variety. _____
2. The *seasons* lengths are all about the same. _____
3. Several *files* were taken from the office. _____
4. The *files* disappearance is a mystery. _____
5. The *students* lockers have been repainted. _____
6. The *students* are responsible for their upkeep. _____
7. No *refunds* or *exchanges* are allowed. _____
8. The *offices* sprinkler *systems* were all set off. _____
9. The *childrens* clothing is on sale. _____

PERSONAL PRONOUNS

A **pronoun** is a word that is used in place of a noun. We use pronouns to avoid using the same noun over and over again.

We would not say, "Lou broke Lou's arm."
We would say, "Lou broke his arm."

Personal pronouns make up the largest group of pronouns. All but one of them refer to people; the other one , "it," refers to a thing. Personal pronouns sometimes change form, depending on how they are used in a sentence. You will learn more about these uses later.

These are the personal pronouns:

Singular	Plural
I, me	we, us
you	you
he, she, it, him, her	they, them

IDENTIFY THE PERSONAL PRONOUNS

Write the pronoun that replaces the noun or nouns in each sentence. Then circle the noun or nouns the pronoun replaces.

1. Fleas are so annoying that most people hate them.

2. Fleas are dangerous because they can carry germs.

3. Some fleas make a buzzing sound as they fly.

4. A flea has a sharp beak that it uses to puncture the skin.

5. The leaping ability of a flea helps it move.

6. "Did you know that a flea can carry disease?" Jess asked Cal.

7. Some circus trainers have caught fleas and trained them.

8. Although training can be done, it is not easy.

9. My friend wonders why he is more bothered by fleas than other people are. _____

10. A person's skin may have swelling and itchiness on it. _____

11. Many people with pets spray them to prevent fleas. _____

12. Frequent cleaning of animals can keep them safe. _____

> Fleas are ugly insects, but as dangerous pests they cannot be ignored. Have any of your pets or farm animals been infected by them? What were the symptoms? How were they treated? You might like to write a composition about the case.

POSSESSIVE PRONOUNS

Possessive pronouns are used to replace possessive nouns. Like possessive nouns, they show ownership, possession, or that one thing is part of another. Possessive pronouns are also noun markers. The possessive forms of pronouns are:
    Singular: my, mine, your, yours, his, her, hers, its
    Plural: our, ours, your, yours, their, theirs
Examples:
    This is *my* locker.
    That is *your* padlock.
    This is *our* classroom.

(Especially note the personal pronoun "it" and the possessive pronoun "its." As with the other pronouns, this is a change of form. Just as "he" and "she" change to "his" and "her," "it" changes to "its." No apostrophe is used.)

Many times possessive pronouns are used by themselves.
Examples:
        Theirs is the red one.
        This dog is not *ours*.
        I have *mine*, but the teacher lost his.

You might be thinking that the meanings of these sentences are not clear. You are right. We use a pronoun only if the noun it refers to is clear. These sample sentences would not be correct all by themselves in a paragraph. They would need other sentences containing nouns to make the pronoun meanings clear.

PART ONE: THE PARTS OF SPEECH

USE THE POSSESSIVE FORM OF PRONOUNS

Replace the italicized words with the correct possessive pronoun.

1. Are these sketches (*belonging to you*)? _____
2. (*belonging to Mandy*) drawings are beautiful. _____
3. This portfolio is (*belonging to me*). _____
4. (*belonging to Heather and me*) paintings are not dry. _____
5. Give me (*belonging to Christine*) drawing. _____
6. (*belonging to Carlos*) is a good example of cubism. _____
7. Listen for clues in (*belonging to Mr. Zoltan*) instructions. _____
8. This sculpture is (*belonging to Joni and me*). _____
9. Can a painting lose (*belonging to a painting*) colour? _____
10. Mrs. Olsen gave (*belonging to several people*) project the most praise. _____
11. My mother bought (*belonging to Ken*) carving. _____
12. (*belonging to Lee and you*) efforts are overlooked. _____
13. The field trip lost (*belonging to the field trip*) appeal. _____

> Look over some of your recent writing. Where have you used pronouns? Have you used any incorrectly? If so, use the help in this exercise to decide what mistakes you have made and correct them.

PRONOUNS AND ANTECEDENTS

A **pronoun** takes the place of a noun. The noun it replaces is called the pronoun's **antecedent**. The word "antecedent" means "coming before." The noun usually comes before the pronoun that replaces it.

    Rosa passed her swimming test. (The pronoun "her" has the antecedent "Rosa.")

Because pronouns are used in the same way as nouns, you won't be surprised to learn that pronouns can be the antecedents of other pronouns.

    He enjoys his new job. (The pronoun "He" is the antecedent of the pronoun "his.")

You know that nouns may be singular or plural. A pronoun must be the same number as the noun it replaces. If the antecedent is singular, the pronoun must also be singular. If the antecedent is plural, the pronoun must also be plural.

    The dog chased its tail. (The singular noun "dog" is replaced by the singular pronoun "its.")
    The doctor treated her patient. (The singular noun "doctor" is replaced by the singular pronoun "her.")
    The generals planned their strategy. (The plural noun "generals" is replaced by the plural pronoun "their.")

Find the antecedents

Write the pronoun in each of the following sentences. Circle its antecedent.

1. Grizzly bears make their homes in western North America.

2. A bear moves its home as the seasons change.

3. Bears are agile, they can stand and walk upright.

4. A bear avoids other bears, but will live with them if there is enough food.

5. A grizzly mates with a female and then leaves her.

6. Grizzlies are omnivorous; they will eat both meat and plants.

7. Dormancy is the period when bears sleep in their dens.

PART ONE: THE PARTS OF SPEECH   17

8. If the winter is long, it causes the bear to remain dormant for a long time.   _____

9. The grizzly can lower its body temperature.   _____

10. If the female is pregnant, she will line the den with branches and boughs.   _____

11. The female will bear the cubs while she is in dormancy.   _____

12. There is a danger that a male will feel threatened by cubs and will kill them.   _____

13. The greatest threat to bears is that their habitats are being taken from them.   _____

14. A bile juice from grizzlies is injected into patients with gallstones and it dissolves them.   _____

> Did you find the last example confusing? That's because there are two possible antecedents in the sentence. Does the pronoun "them" refer to the patients or the gallstones? How would you rewrite the sentence to make it clear?

DEMONSTRATIVE AND INTERROGATIVE PRONOUNS

When people demonstrate, they draw attention to themselves or to something they are explaining. **Demonstrative pronouns** are used for a similar purpose. They point to something. If the people or things they point to are nearby in space or time, we use:

Singular	Plural
this	these

If the people or things are farther away, we use:

that	those

Examples:
  This is my book. (nearby)   *That* is your book. (farther away)
  These are the new skis.   *Those* are the old skis.

You use demonstrative pronouns often in speaking or writing.

USE DEMONSTRATIVE PRONOUNS

Write a correct demonstrative pronoun to begin each sentence below.

1. _____ is the first sushi bar I've ever visited.

2. _____ are my favourite fish.

3. _____ doesn't taste as I thought it would.

4. _____ was a great idea you had.

5. _____ are the friends I want you to meet.

6. _____ chopsticks over there are yours.

7. _____ is our car in the parking lot across the street.

INTERROGATIVE PRONOUNS

A question sentence is sometimes called an **interrogative sentence**. To "interrogate" means to question. **Interrogative pronouns** are used to ask questions. The interrogative pronouns are "who," "whom," "whose," "which," and "what."
Examples:
    What are you wearing?
    Which do you prefer?
    Who is the president?
    Whom did you elect?
    Whose mother baked the cookies?

IDENTIFY DEMONSTRATIVE AND INTERROGATIVE PRONOUNS

Write whether the italicized pronoun is demonstrative or interrogative.

1. *Who* delivered the package? _____

2. Are *these* the shirts you ordered? _____

3. I did not choose *that* colour. _____

4. *Which* of the shirts do you like best? _____

5. *What* was the cost? _____

6. Maria preferred *those*. _____

7. *This* is the ugliest thing I've ever seen. _____

PART ONE: THE PARTS OF SPEECH

8. *Whose* is the red polka dot one? _____

9. *Whom* should we blame for this mess? _____

10. *Who* was home alone last night? _____

The words we use as demonstrative and interrogative pronouns can also be used in other ways. You will learn what these uses are later. When you learn more about sentences, it will be quite clear how the word is being used.

INDEFINITE PRONOUNS

Indefinite pronouns are different from personal pronouns because they do not refer to a specific person or thing. Some indefinite pronouns are singular.

another	each	everything	one
anybody	either	neither	somebody
anyone	everybody	nobody	someone
anything	everyone	no one	

Contrast these pronouns with the demonstrative pronouns in the last exercise. You will see that demonstrative pronouns specify something exact (*this* hat, *those* boots); whereas indefinite pronouns are quite vague. Also note that indefinite pronouns usually stand by themselves; they are not noun markers. (*Either* and *neither* may be noun markers or may stand alone.)

Some indefinite pronouns are plural.

all   both   few   many   several

Example: *Many* of the viewers expressed their opinions. *Several* voiced their anger.

Use indefinite pronouns correctly

Write the indefinite pronoun. Then circle the correct possessive pronoun.

1. Nobody lost (his or her, their) place. _____

2. Everyone has paid (his or her, their) admission. _____

3. Many of the musicians entered with (his or her, their) instruments. _____

4. Each of the groups has (its, their) own manager. _____

5. All of the musicians practised (his or her, their) numbers. _____

6. Neither of the girls brought (her, their) eyeglasses. _____

7. If anyone has an extra ticket, have (him or her, them) see me. _____

8. Several of the banks of lights were missing (its, their) bulbs. _____

9. Both of the opening groups pleased (its, their) fans. _____

10. Neither of the boys brought (his, their) autograph book. _____

11. Everything was blasting at (its, their) loudest level. _____

12. Some of the ushers called in (his or her, their) security guards. _____

13. None of the music was played at (its, their) normal volume. _____

14. No one offered (his or her, their) help. _____

15. Either of the girls can explain (her, their) disappointment. _____

Note: It is becoming quite common in conversational English to use the plural possessive "their" after the singular indefinite pronoun "everyone." People use "their" to avoid the awkward-sounding use of "his" or "her." In formal written English, however, the singular possessive should be used with the singular indefinite pronoun.

Example:
    Everyone has *his* or *her* ticket.   (correct)
    Everyone has *their* ticket.   (incorrect)

The sentence could be rewritten to avoid the problem.
    They all have *their* tickets.
    We all have *our* tickets.

PRONOUNS AND NOUN MARKERS

"Them" and "Those"

"Those" is a possessive pronoun and is used as a noun marker. "Them" is a personal pronoun. The words cannot be used in place of each other.
Correct:
    Kim bought *those* jeans.
    (The possessive pronoun "those" marks the noun "jeans.")
    Kim bought *them*.
    (The pronoun "them" follows the verb "bought.")
Incorrect:
    Kim bought them jeans. (Unless you mean Kim bought jeans for them.)

"Here" and "There"

The word "here" includes the idea of "this." The word "there" includes the idea of "that." Therefore, it is incorrect to say, "this here" or "that there."
Correct:
    Luis chose this book.   Sami chose that book.
Incorrect:
    Luis chose this here book.   Sami chose that there book.

"Kind" and "Sort"

These words may suggest the idea of more than one thing, but they are singular in form. If you wish to use a possessive pronoun with them you must use the singular form "this" or "that." If you use the word "kinds" or "sorts," then you are using the plural form. You would then use the plural possessive pronouns, "these" or "those."
    This kind of material is warm.   *Those* kinds of hats are stylish.

Use pronouns and noun markers correctly

Circle the correct word for each sentence.
1. Nina knows (them, those) artists.
2. (That, Those) kind of painting is very popular.
3. Saul gave Amy (that, that there) portfolio.
4. Our teacher likes (this, these) kinds of sculptures.
5. Mr. Barker carved (them, those) figures.
6. May I borrow (this, this here) table?
7. (This, These) kind of paint costs less.
8. Camille uses (that, those) kind of brush.
9. Should I throw away (this, this here) paper?
10. (Them, Those) brush strokes are unusual.
11. (That, That there) colour does not match.

12. (Them, Those) comments are not helpful.
13. (That, Those) sort of criticism hurts.
14. Ashley never makes (that, those) kinds of remarks.
15. Put (these, these here) easels away.
16. (Them, Those) clothes need cleaning.
17. (This, These) type of paper is sold in art supply stores.
18. Can we visit (that, that there) art gallery?
19. Jennifer wore one of (them, those) smocks to cover her clothing.
20. I don't like (that, those) style of painting.

REVIEW: USING PRONOUNS

USE PRONOUNS CORRECTLY

Write the correct pronoun in each sentence.

1. Has (he, him) seen the program?
2. Has Ms. Benigni given (they, them) the exam?
3. I always enjoy listening to (she, her).
4. Hand me (them, those) nails, please.
5. (This, That) is my house on the next corner.
6. Someone lost (his or her, their) padlock.
7. Anyone can enter (his or her, their) project in the science fair.
8. Several of the customers returned (his or her, their) apples.
9. Some of the jewelry lost (their, its) shine.
10. Both of the dancers gave me (his or her, their) autographs.
11. Did you order one of (them, those) T-shirts?

Part One: The Parts of Speech

Identify the Antecedents

Write each pronoun. Circle its antecedent.

1. Hal entered the room. It was dark. _____
2. Betsy turned on her flashlight. _____
3. Hal wondered if he was in the wrong room. _____
4. Did you check the address, Betsy? _____
5. The two young people never returned to tell their story. _____

Rewrite each of the following sentences

If the nouns and pronouns are singular, rewrite them as plural. If they are plural, rewrite them as singular. Be sure to make pronouns agree with their antecedents. Make any other changes in the sentence that are necessary so that the new sentence is correct.

1. She lost her map somewhere back along the trail.
   _____

2. Their shoes were kept inside their tents.
   _____

3. The bears roamed near the camps at night.
   _____

4. His compass showed that the river was to his left.
   _____

5. Some people thought that the logger's cabin was haunted.
   _____

HOW TO IDENTIFY VERBS

Verbs are often the key words in a sentence. If you can find the verb, the rest of the sentence usually falls into place. Unfortunately, verbs are tricky. Sometimes they are one word, sometimes they are two or even three words. When verbs are made up of more than one word, sometimes another word comes between the parts of the verb. Luckily, you already know how to use verbs. You use verbs every day when you speak or listen or read, and of course when you write.

Here are two ideas to remember about verbs: they often show *action* and they show *time*. Verbs show the action that is being done by the person, place or thing referred to by a noun.

> The Concorde *landed* in Paris. (The verb "landed" shows what the noun "Concorde" did.)

The verb also shows if the events we are talking about in the sentence are taking place now, have already taken place, or will take place.

As you know, there are three times: past, present, and future.
Tell the time of each of these sentences.

> Donovan *ran* for our track team.
> Maria *plays* for the school hockey team.
> Our school band *will perform* at the next assembly.

The word that told you the time was the verb.

For each of the sentences above, change the time to two other times. Change only the verb; do not add any other words except the ones you need to make the verb correct.

Now you know how to identify the verb in any sentence. Just change the time of the sentence; the word that changes is the verb. If more than one word changes, those words are probably parts of the verb.

The time a verb shows is called the **verb tense**. Just as there are three times, so there are three main verb tenses: past tense, present tense, and future tense.

Identify verbs and verb tenses

In each sentence, write the verb and the time or tense of the verb.

1. My friend studies dreams.   _____

   _____

2. I forgot most of my dreams.   _____

   _____

3. You will remember dreams sometimes.

4. Dreams contain symbols.

5. Often, the events in a dream mean something else.

6. I will dream of flying.

7. I tried to escape from something.

8. Dreams will have sudden changes of time.

9. The setting of my dream revealed some inner childhood fears.

10. The people seem like strangers to me.

11. Nightmares will frighten the dreamer.

12. Children often woke up screaming.

13. Some children thought dreams were real events.

14. Some mental illnesses were
    helped by studying the patient's
    dreams.   _____

                                               _____

15. Carl Jung wrote a book about the
    meanings of dreams.   _____

                                               _____

Did you notice that some of the sentences had a verb that was made up of two words? You still knew the time of the sentence; that is, you knew the tense of the verb.

The sentences in the exercise are all on the same topic, but all the changing tenses make them hard to understand. Changing only the verbs, rewrite the sentences so that they are easier to read. Not all the sentences need to be in the same tense. Decide which tense or time makes the most sense. That will depend on the content of the sentence.

1. _____
2. _____
3. _____
4. _____
5. _____
6. _____
7. _____
8. _____
9. _____
10. _____
11. _____
12. _____
13. _____
14. _____
15. _____

PART ONE: THE PARTS OF SPEECH

THE PARTS OF A VERB

Most of the verbs that we use are made up of two or more words. The **main verb** is the one that tells most about what the noun does or is. The other verb parts are called **helping verbs**. Sometimes there may be two helping verbs in the same sentence. The helping verb is usually a small word that goes along with the main verb.

Helping verbs are usually one of four types:
1) Forms of "be":   is, are, was, were
2) Forms of "have":   has, had, have
3) Forms of "do":   do, does, did
4) Forms of "would": will, would

Because they are part of the verb, they change if the time of the sentence changes. So to find all parts of the verb, do the same as you did before. Just change the time of the sentence (that is, change the tense of the verb). The words that change will be the verbs.

Some main verbs will not change form when you change the time, but the helping verbs will.

Identify main verbs and helping verbs

Circle the verb in each sentence. Be sure to include the helping verbs. State the tense of each verb.

1. Many people are frightened by bats. _____
2. People have found bats in all parts of the world. _____
3. Bats were eating mostly fruit, flower stems, and leaves. _____
4. Only a few bats have drunk blood. _____
5. None of the bats in Canada are called vampire bats. _____
6. Bats will hang upside down in dark places during the day. _____
7. A bat has seldom flown into a person's hair. _____
8. Vampire bats did cause some harm to animals. _____
9. A vampire bat will drink about 20 mL of blood each night. _____
10. They are going back to the same animal each night. _____

11. The animal is losing too little blood to become sick. _____

12. The animal sometimes is infected in the open wound. _____

13. Vampire bats have never attacked a human. _____

14. Biologists did find anti-clotting ingredients in the vampire bat's saliva. _____

15. The ingredients have helped humans. _____

> As with the previous exercise, these sentences are all on the same topic, but they seem odd when you read them all together. Changing only the verbs, rewrite the sentences so that they are easier to read. Change only the verbs that need to be changed to make the sentences easier to understand. If you wish, use the sentences as the basis for a composition on bats.

> Read over a recent composition you have written. Find the helping verbs and the main verbs that you used in some of your sentences. This shows that you already know how to use these verbs. Now you know what they are called.

VERB TENSES

So far we have looked at simple verb tenses—past, present, and future. These simple tenses are often not enough to express an idea. For example, you could think about two things that happened in the past, but one happened before the other. A simple past tense will not express this idea. Suppose you want to say that you arrived at Tyler's house and that when you got there, Tyler had already eaten his lunch. If you use only a simple past tense, you would write:

> I arrived at Tyler's house. He ate his lunch.

This does not express the meaning you want. You could write:

> I arrived at Tyler's house. He had eaten his lunch.

(You might also decide to combine the two sentences into one. We will study those kinds of sentences later in this book.)

The tense in the second sentence of the second example is called the **past perfect**. It is called *past* because the action occurred in the past. It is called *perfect* because the action in the second sentence was complete before the action in the first sentence occurred. The word "perfect" in this context means "complete." This is another complicated explanation of something that you already know how to use. Now you just need to learn what the tenses are called so that you can discuss your compositions more accurately.

PART ONE: THE PARTS OF SPEECH   29

To express an action that was complete before another action occurred, we use the **perfect tense**. The perfect tense may be used in the present and in the future as well as in the past.

Present Tense	He lives.	You learn.
Past Tense	He lived.	You learned.
Future Tense	He will live.	You will learn.
Present Perfect Tense	He has lived.	You have learned.
Past Perfect Tense	He had lived.	You had learned.
Future Perfect Tense	He will have lived.	You will have learned.

Notice that the tense of the verb is shown by the helping verb. The helping verb is some form of the verb "to have": has, have, had. For example, in the present perfect tense, the helping verb is in the present tense, "has." In the past, it is "had." In the future, it is "will have." Use these example sentences as a guide in doing the exercise below.

Recognize verb tenses

Underline the verb in each sentence. Write the tense of each verb.

1. Wendy has taken Spanish for two years.   _____

2. Edson will fail the test for sure.   _____

3. I had forgotten everything about grammar.   _____

4. Lou has two grammar-checking programs.   _____

5. The teacher checked us in.   _____

6. By next week, Carla will have been here for six months.   _____

7. The two-hour exams will tire us.   _____

8. Tony had brought an extra bottle of water.   _____

9. Katri filled two exam books.   _____

10. We have finished the exercise.   _____

Use verb tenses

Write a sentence for each of the verbs below. Use the tense indicated.

1. read (past)

    _____

2. talk (future)

    _____

3. finish (present perfect)
   _____

4. smile (present)
   _____

5. hope (past perfect)
   _____

6. leave (future perfect)
   _____

THE PRINCIPAL PARTS OF A VERB

The **principal parts** of a verb are the basic forms from which all the verb tenses can be made. You already know two of the principal parts—the present and the past. A third form is called the **past participle**. The past participle is the part that is used with a helping verb. The past participle is used for perfect tenses like the ones you studied in the previous exercise.

Most verbs form the past tense and the past participle by adding "d" or "ed" to the present tense form. Note that any form of the helping verb "have" could be used (i.e., has, had).

Present	Past	Past Participle
arrive	arrived	(have) arrived
burn	burned	(have) burned
drop	dropped	(have) dropped
bury	buried	(have) buried

(Notice that some verbs change their spelling when "d" or "ed" is added.)

Verbs that form the participle in this way are called **regular verbs** because they are the most common form.

Form the principal parts of regular verbs

Using the list of examples as a guide, write the principal parts of the following verbs.

Present   Past   Past Participle

1. appear   _____   _____
2. shop   _____   _____
3. open   _____   _____

PART ONE: THE PARTS OF SPEECH   31

Present	Past	Past Participle
4. carry	_____	_____
5. travel	_____	_____
6. praise	_____	_____
7. tip	_____	_____
8. change	_____	_____
9. close	_____	_____
10. trap	_____	_____
11. order	_____	_____
12. compare	_____	_____
13. snap	_____	_____
14. cry	_____	_____
15. describe	_____	_____

LINKING VERBS

Most verbs show action or time. However, there is a small group of verbs that show time, but do not show action. Some verbs simply link a word in the first part of the sentence (usually a noun) to a word in the last part of the sentence (usually a noun or adjective). These are called **linking verbs**. The most common linking verbs are forms of the verb "to be": is, are, was, were.

> That car is a Saab. (The verb "is" links the two nouns "car" and "Saab.")
> My answers were all correct. (The verb "were" links the noun "answers" and the adjective "correct.")

You will notice that these forms of "to be" are also used as helping verbs, which we studied earlier. When these words are used as helpers, there is always another main verb with them. The main verb will show the action of the noun or pronoun. When they are linking verbs, they are used alone.

Some linking verbs seem to show action.
Examples:
> seem, remain, taste, smell, sound, appear, look, feel
> become, go, grow, turn, make

"Grow," "go," "turn" and "make" seem like actions. But in some sentences these words only link two parts of the sentences.
Example:
> The animals *grow* restless at feeding time. (In this sentence, there is no action of growing. The word "grow" just links the words "animals" and "restless." We could also write, *The animals are restless at feeding time.*)

IDENTIFY LINKING VERBS

Write the linking verbs in each sentence. Circle the two words that are connected by the linking verb.

1. The names for the days of the week are interesting. _____
2. Sunday was a day to worship the sun. _____
3. Moonday was a Norse day of moon worship. _____
4. That name became Monday. _____
5. Tiu, Woden, and Thor were Viking gods. _____
6. Their names are now the names of days. _____
7. Friggas was the Norse goddess of love. _____
8. Her name has become Friday. _____
9. Saturn was the Roman god of the sun. _____
10. Saturn's day is now Saturday. _____

DETERMINE THE LINKING VERBS

In each pair of sentences, there is one linking verb. Circle the verbs that are linking verbs.

1. My uncle grows potatoes. My uncle grows angry sometimes.
2. I can taste apples in this drink. This drink tastes odd.
3. The cars remain in the lot until the gate is opened. The animals remain quiet in the hot weather.
4. Andy feels sick. The cloth feels smooth and rich.
5. I make bread in the bread machine. That makes ten dollars that we have collected.

CONTRACTIONS AND POSSESSIVE PRONOUNS

One cause of pronoun problems is that certain words sound the same but are spelled differently and have different uses. The problem usually arises with **contractions**. Contractions are much more common in spoken language than in written language; and, of course, in spoken language we don't have to worry about spelling. If we are not careful, spoken language can create problems in written language. Here are some common problem words.

  its/it's   their/they're
  whose/who's   your/you're

PART ONE: THE PARTS OF SPEECH

As you look at each pair, notice that one of the words is a possessive pronoun and the other is a contraction of a pronoun and a linking verb. These are two very different uses, so if you think about the structure of the sentence, you should have no trouble deciding which is correct.

The dog hurt its paw. (possessive)
The dog whines to show that it's hurt. (contraction of the pronoun subject "it" and the linking verb "is")

USE THE CORRECT WORD

Write the correct word for each sentence.

1. (Who's, Whose) in charge here?
2. May I see (your, you're) ID?
3. (Its, It's) too late to get in.
4. (Their, They're) tickets have been paid for.
5. (Who's, Whose) fault was that?
6. The rave has lost (its, it's) appeal.
7. We saw (their, they're) car outside.
8. (Its, It's) roar could be heard all over the zoo.
9. (Their, They're) always talking about (their, they're) new clothes.
10. (Who's, Whose) going to decide (who's, whose) house we go to?

IRREGULAR VERBS (1)

You probably guessed that if there are regular verbs, there must also be irregular verbs. The reason all verbs are not formed the same way is that our language was not put together as one logical piece. The English language contains many words that were adopted from other languages. Also, English has changed over the years. Some old forms have been dropped, but others have been kept. Language is created by human beings as they go about their everyday activities. This has happened for centuries and in many parts of the world. So English is not entirely regular. In Part One of the companion volume of this book, *Irwin Writing Skills*, there is some information about the sources of Canadian English and about the different ways of using it.

You know how to use these verbs, but it will help to learn how they are formed. For convenience, we can group these irregular verbs into five basic patterns. We will study these patterns over the next few pages.

Group 1. Some irregular verbs keep the same form for all three principal parts.

Present	Past	Past Participle
burst	burst	(have) burst
cost	cost	(have) cost
put	put	(have) put
set	set	(have) set

Group 2. Some irregular verbs change form only once. The past and the past participle are the same.

Present	Past	Past Participle
bring	brought	(have) brought
catch	caught	(have) caught
lead	led	(have) led
lend	lent	(have) lent
lose	lost	(have) lost
say	said	(have) said
sit	sat	(have) sat

Use irregular verbs

Circle the correct verb form from the two given.
1. Leanna (putted, put) the final touches on our project.
2. Mr. Gallo has (lent, lended) us the tape.
3. Georgio (brang, brought) the boards for the frame.
4. The materials (cost, costed) fifty dollars.
5. The judges have (setted, set) the standards for the fair.
6. Our staff advisor (sayed, said) we had done a good job.
7. Our review had not (catched, caught) any mistakes.
8. The chief judge (led, lead) the group into the room.
9. Our parents (sat, sitted) in the stands.
10. One of our water dams (bursted, burst).
11. Nick (lead, led) the group out of the room.
12. That's the third time our projects have (losted, lost).

> Look over some of your recent writing. Find some regular verbs that you have used. Then find some irregular verbs. Have you used the parts correctly?

IRREGULAR VERBS (2)

Group 3. Verbs in this group add "n" or "en" to the past tense to form the past participle.

Present	Past	Past Participle
break	broke	(have) broken
choose	chose	(have) chosen
freeze	froze	(have) frozen
speak	spoke	(have) spoken
steal	stole	(have) stolen
wear	wore	(have) worn

USE THE IRREGULAR VERBS

Circle the correct form of the verb.
1. The class had (chose, chosen) Lukas as the delegate.
2. The previous delegate has (wore, worn) out his welcome.
3. The committee was (froze, frozen) on one topic.
4. The new delegate (spoke, spoken) to the council.
5. No one has (stole, stolen) any sleep in class lately.
6. Colin (broke, broken) the record for late arrivals.
7. Nisha (wore, worn) her gold medal to the assembly.

Group 4. The verbs in this group change their final vowels. The vowel changes from "i" in the present tense to "a" in the past tense and "u" in the past participle.

Present	Past	Past Participle
begin	began	(have) begun
drink	drank	(have) drunk
ring	rang	(have) rung
sing	sang	(have) sung
swim	swam	(have) swum

USE THE IRREGULAR VERBS

Write the correct form of the verb.
1. Angelo (drunk, drank) two bottles of water. _____
2. Vanessa has (swum, swam) across the river. _____
3. I (sung, sang) in the school musical last year. _____
4. The phone has not (rang, rung) all day. _____
5. We (begun, began) to think you were not coming. _____

6. Jody has (sang, sung) on local television. _____

7. The graduation ceremony had already (began, begun). _____

You may have noticed that irregular verbs are some of the most common verbs we use. These verbs are among the oldest in our language, and they retain some of the old forms. Newer verbs are usually regular. For example, if you were to invent a verb, "snurf," the principal parts would be regular: "snurf," "snurfed," "have snurfed."

IRREGULAR VERBS (3)

Group 5. These verbs form the past participle from the present tense form.

Present	Past	Past Participle
come	came	(have) come
do	did	(have) done
eat	ate	(have) eaten
fall	fell	(have) fallen
give	gave	(have) given
go	went	(have) gone
grow	grew	(have) grown
know	knew	(have) known
ride	rode	(have) ridden
run	ran	(have) run
see	saw	(have) seen
take	took	(have) taken
throw	threw	(have) thrown
write	wrote	(have) written

USE THE IRREGULAR VERBS

Using the above table as a guide, write the correct verb form for each sentence below.

1. I have (gave, given) your suggestion some thought. _____

2. Tiana's idea (fell, fallen) on deaf ears. _____

3. Ryan had already (threw, thrown) his proposal out. _____

4. Three groups have (went, gone) to the Metro Zoo. _____

5. Have you (saw, seen) what happened? _____

6. The young gorilla has (grew, grown) much larger. _____

Part One: The Parts of Speech   37

7. It must have (ate, eaten) plenty of food. _____

8. We (rode, ridden) the zoomobile to the polar bear enclosure. _____

9. Camela has (took, taken) some great photos. _____

10. Who (did, done) the developing? _____

11. Kelvin has (ran, run) these tours before. _____

12. Has the bus (came, come) yet? _____

13. Jeffrey had (knew, known) the trip would be fun. _____

14. Ms. Kristich has (wrote, written) a recommendation for us. _____

15. The other group had (gone, went) to the Science Centre. _____

16. An advisor (seen, saw) them enter a restricted area. _____

17. Naomi had (fell, fallen) and sprained her ankle. _____

18. The security guard (taken, took) them back to the staff member in charge. _____

> These are the five groups of irregular verbs. Mistakes are often made with these past participles because they do not follow the regular pattern, and also because they are quite different from each other. They are best learned by careful use and by noting their use in reading material. As you are reading a magazine, a newspaper, a novel, or a textbook, look for irregular verbs and note their use.

> You might find it helpful to keep your own list of irregular verbs that cause you trouble. Write the three principal parts of each verb and check back over your list often. Soon you will have mastered them.

REVIEW: USING VERBS

After you complete each exercise below, stop and discuss your answers before going on to the next exercise. Describe the use of these verbs. Why did you choose the form you did? By putting our understanding into words, we often clarify our thoughts.

RECOGNIZE VERBS

Circle the verb in each sentence.
1. Sir John Franklin searched for the Northwest Passage.
2. The Panama Canal links the Atlantic and Pacific oceans in the south.
3. Could a passage like that exist in the north?
4. The expedition challenged the ice and extreme cold of the Arctic.
5. Two years passed without any message from the expedition.
6. The British government offered a reward for its discovery.
7. The search parties explored many parts of the Arctic.
8. For many years they found no trace of Franklin's expedition.

USE VERBS CORRECTLY

Circle the correct form of each verb in parentheses.
1. In 1851, a search party had (find, found) a supply of canned goods and bottles.
2. Franklin's expedition (was, were) gone.
3. They also (find, found) three graves.
4. The men had (froze, frozen) to death.
5. They had not (saw, seen) any trace of Franklin's route.
6. All hope had been (lose, lost) for them by 1854.
7. Nine months later, a doctor had (buy, bought) some items from natives.
8. The Natives had (met, meet) several men from the mainland years earlier.
9. The men (are, were) not Natives.
10. The Natives had (hear, heard) shots in the springtime when geese arrived.
11. Lady Franklin (buy, bought) a schooner for a final search.
12. This expedition was (led, lead) by Francis McClintock.
13. The Franklin expedition (was, were) lost forever.

Circle the verb in each sentence.
1. A note had been found by W.R. Hobson, one of McClintock's men.
2. In 1848, Franklin had abandoned his two ships.
3. They had been trapped by ice for several months.

4. Hobson found two skeletons in a small boat.
5. The survivors had started a death march to the south.

> Look up some information on this great mystery of Franklin's Expedition. You might like to write about it. The story is so interesting, your composition might be expository, descriptive, or narrative. Or you could write an imaginary letter that one of Franklin's men had written to his wife and family.

USING ADJECTIVES

Adjectives modify nouns or pronouns. When you modify a car or a stereo system, you make changes in it. The word "modify" means "to change." The words we call **modifiers** in grammar change the meanings of the words they modify.
Example:
>The dog barked.

There are no modifiers in this sentence. We could be talking about any dog and any kind of barking.
Example:
>The *brown* dog barked *fiercely*.

We have added two modifiers. One tells a little more about the dog and the other tells something about how it barked.
Example:
>The *little brown* dog *on the porch* barked *fiercely, with a squeaky yapping sound*.

Now we know a lot more about the dog and how it barked.

The modifiers we added in the sample sentences are **adjectives** and **adverbs**. We will study adjectives in this exercise. Notice that one-word adjectives appear between the noun marker and the noun. In the example, "little" and "brown" appear between "the" and "dog." The phrase "on the porch" is also an adjective, even though it is a group of words. We will study adjective phrases later.

Adjectives can tell us three things about nouns or pronouns:
>1) What kind? (*small* sweater, *purple* crayon)
>2) Which one or ones? (*those* apples, *that* house, *this* car)
>3) How many or how much? (*all* girls, *little* time, *sixty* kilograms)

The adjectives in examples 2 and 3 are also pronouns and noun markers. When we studied noun markers, we examined the use of articles—a, an, the. Those articles are often classed as adjectives.

Some adjectives are formed from proper nouns and are called **proper adjectives**. Just as proper nouns are written with a capital letter, so are proper adjectives. Examples:

Proper Noun	Proper Adjective
Canada	Canadian
France	French
England	English

In sentences with linking verbs, an adjective could appear after the verb. In these sentences, the adjective still modifies the noun that comes before the verb.
> That dog is *black*.
> Your jacket is *fashionable*.

RECOGNIZE ADJECTIVES

Circle the adjectives in these sentences.
1. The giant Pacific octopus lives in cold, northern waters.
2. These unusual animals seek out sunken ships, or dark caves with narrow openings.
3. Octopuses are gray, brown, or reddish.
4. These huge, boneless creatures can slip through tiny openings.
5. Their powerful arms contain suction cups to grasp their prey.
6. Frightened octopuses use jet propulsion to make a fast escape.
7. They also eject a slimy, black ink that acts like a smoke screen.
8. Larger fish prey upon young octopuses.
9. A fully-grown octopus has few enemies other than humans.

There are 29 adjectives in the sentences above, not counting articles. Did you find them all?

ADJECTIVES IN COMPARISONS

When we compare one thing with another, we use the **comparative form** of adjectives. To make this form, we add "er" to short adjectives or use the word "more" with longer adjectives.
> Michelle is *taller* than Fernando.
> Amanda is the *youngest* child in her family.
> Apples are *more plentiful* than pears.
> Nikki is the *most talented musician* in the group.

When we compare one thing with more than one other, we use the **superlative form** of adjectives. We add "est" to short adjectives or use the word "most" with longer adjectives. Here are some examples.

PART ONE: THE PARTS OF SPEECH

Adjective	Comparative	Superlative
old	older	oldest
slim	slimmer	slimmest
green	greener	greenest
poor	poorer	poorest
pretty	prettier	prettiest
lovely	lovelier	loveliest
courageous	more courageous	most courageous
expensive	more expensive	most expensive
interesting	more interesting	most interesting

Use the word "other" when you compare something with everything else of its kind.
> Mr. De Paulo is more patient than any *other* teacher.
> (It is unclear to say, "Mr. De Paulo is more patient than any teacher." This sentence does not make clear that Mr. De Paulo is also a teacher.)

Use either the "er" or "est" forms or the "more," "most" form. Do not use both.
> Example: Kate is more bigger than John. (incorrect)
> Kate is bigger than John. (correct)

Here are a few irregular adjectives.

good	better	best
well	better	best
bad	worse	worst
little	less or lesser	least
many	more	most
much	more	most

Often, the answer to grammar problems is in your own head. Stop and think about what you mean, the idea you want to express. You will often be able to think of the correct word yourself.

USE ADJECTIVES IN COMPARISONS

If the comparison is correct, write "correct." If the comparison is incorrect, write the correct form.

1. Prince Edward Island is the smallest province. _____
2. McIntosh apples are the better of all apples. _____
3. They are my most favouritest snack. _____
4. Canadian apples are more tastier than imported apples. _____

5. This exercise is easier than the last one. _____

6. Our school's team is gooder than your school's. _____

7. That is the baddest cheer I have ever heard. _____

8. The floral display is the attractivest of all. _____

9. Sal is the tallest of the two boys. _____

10. English is spoken in more countries than any language. _____

USING ADVERBS

Another kind of modifier is the **adverb**. Adverbs have more uses than adjectives. Adverbs can modify verbs, adjectives, or other adverbs. Adverbs may appear in different parts of a sentence.

Type 1. Adverbs that modify verbs.
Adverbs often tell *how*, *when*, *where*, or *why* the action expressed by the verb occurred.

Tickets sold *quickly*. (How?)
The director lives *nearby*. (Where?)
The group arrives *tomorrow*. (When?)
Quietly, the thief approached.
The thief *quietly* approached.
The thief approached *quietly*.

Adverbs that tell *why* are usually phrases or clauses, which we will study later.

Type 2. Adverbs that modify adjectives.
When adverbs modify adjectives, they occur before the adjective—with one exception. The only adverb that comes after the adjective is "enough."

That was a *very* funny show.
The star was *extremely* talented.
The dancers were *so* good!
The audience was *unusually* large.
They are good *enough* to turn professional.

Type 3. Adverbs that modify other adverbs.
When adverbs modify other adverbs they appear before the adverb, with the same exception as is noted above.

He snores *really* loudly.
We slept *pretty* soundly.
Our friends complained often *enough* to be heard.

PART ONE: THE PARTS OF SPEECH

Types 2 and 3 are sometimes called **intensifiers**. They intensify the meanings of the adjectives or adverbs they modify. Notice that most of these adverbs are not really descriptive. They add very little to the meaning of the adjectives they modify. Good writers are careful not to use them too often.

RECOGNIZE ADVERBS

Circle the adverbs in the following sentences. Indicate whether each modifies a verb, an adjective, or another adverb.

1. The Premier signed the bill recently. _____
2. The numerous clauses were examined very carefully. _____
3. The opposition members loudly expressed their disapproval. _____
4. Daily, the newspaper stories criticized the bill. _____
5. Almost every member spoke passionately during the debate. _____
6. Pretty nearly every citizen will be affected. _____
7. A deeply felt issue was at stake. _____
8. Demonstrators quietly walked outside. _____
9. Heavily armed security guards kept a grimly silent watch. _____
10. The government's carefully organized plan worked well. _____
11. The costs of the provisions in the bill had been calculated repeatedly. _____
12. By next year the highly controversial law will be in effect. _____
13. Soon every student will be paid to stay in school. _____
14. An incredibly large salary will be paid. _____
15. Teachers are sharply critical of the plan. _____
16. Tuition fees will be eliminated immediately. _____

17. Students will be quite wealthy. _____

18. The last few sentences are completely false. _____

The sentences above contain 24 adverbs. Did you find them all?

You must be careful when identifying adverbs that modify adjectives. Remember that more than one adjective can be used at a time. In some sentences, there may be two or more words before a noun. Some or all of these may be adjectives or some could be adverbs. You will have no trouble if you think about which word each of these words is modifying. It will be clear that adjectives modify nouns, while adverbs modify the adjectives.

ADVERBS IN COMPARISONS

Comparisons using adverbs work very much the same as comparisons using adjectives. We use adverbs in comparison when we want to compare one or more actions. When we want to compare an action with one other, we use the **comparative form** of the adverb. We add "er" to most short adverbs. We use "more" with most adverbs that end in "ly."

Dana ran *faster* than Jill.
The motor runs *more smoothly* now.

When we compare one action with two or more others, we use the **superlative form**. We add "est" to most short adverbs and use "most" with most longer adverbs.

Ryan sang the *loudest* of all.
This level is the *most advanced* course offered.

Use the word "other" when you compare one action with every other action of its kind.

My mother works longer hours than any *other* manager.
(It is unclear to say, "My mother works longer hours than any manager."
This sentence does not make clear that your mother is a manager.)

Do not use "er" with "more," or "est" with "most." Use one form or the other; but not both.

most costliest (incorrect)
costliest (correct)

Here are some unusual adverb comparisons.

Adverb	Comparative	Superlative
well	better	best
much	more	most
little	less	least
far	farther	farthest

PART ONE: THE PARTS OF SPEECH   45

USE ADVERBS IN COMPARISONS

If the comparison is correct, write "correct." If the comparison is incorrect, write the correct form.

1. Natalia dived the most gracefully of all the divers. _____

2. Our swim team performed more better than the other teams. _____

3. Our coach taught more thoroughly than any coach. _____

4. We go to swim meets more oftener than other schools do. _____

5. Of the three events, this one lasts longer. _____

6. Our relay team swims bestest of all. _____

7. This year's team competes more strongly than last year's team. _____

8. We went farthest in the competition than your team did. _____

9. This type of dive tests divers better than any event. _____

10. Our team relaxed most completely than they had in weeks. _____

ADJECTIVE OR ADVERB?

Adjectives	Adverbs
modify nouns	modify verbs, adjectives, or adverbs
if single word, appear between marker and noun	may appear anywhere in sentence
may tell *which one, what kind*	may tell *where, when, how* about verb
may tell *how many* about noun or pronoun	may be used as intensifiers with adjectives or adverbs

USE MODIFIERS

Circle the modifiers in each sentence. Tell whether each is an adjective or an adverb. Be prepared to explain your choice. Some of these sentences are more complex than the simple ones we have studied so far. However, the adjectives and adverbs are used in the same ways.

1. The visitor spoke quietly to us. _____

2. She was pleasant but firm. _____

3. The woman told interesting stories about the world's supply of food. _____

4. She gave a very thoughtful account of horrible famine and extravagant wealth. _____

5. The world's greatest problem today may be food supply. _____

6. Third-world nations are much poorer than other nations. _____

7. World population is growing rapidly every year. _____

8. The need for food is enormous. _____

9. In nearly every country, lucky people have enough food. _____

10. Those less fortunate are always hungry. _____

11. Temperate parts of the world have a very good climate for farming. _____

12. The population grows more slowly in wealthy countries. _____

13. The soil is poorer and drier in most developing countries. _____

14. An adequate supply of calories is needed by the human body. _____

15. Protein is vital for health. _____

16. If there are insufficient calories, the human body changes protein into the necessary energy. _____

17. Less protein is used to build body cells. _____

18. The terrible result is massive starvation. _____

19. Perhaps 600 million people have protein starvation. _____

20. These people urgently need our help. _____

In these sentences, many words that look like nouns are used as adjectives. It is how the word is used in a particular sentence that determines its part of speech.

PART ONE: THE PARTS OF SPEECH 47

> What can be done about world hunger? Can a high-school student do anything about starving people half a world away? Perhaps some students in your school have experienced daily hunger. Investigate world hunger at your school or local library or on the Internet.

ADJECTIVES AND ADVERBS TO NOTE

"Good" and "Well." "Good" is always an adjective. It modifies a noun or a pronoun.

    Habib is a *good* friend.   This drink is *good* and hot.

"Well" can be either an adjective or an adverb. As an adjective, "well" means "in good health." In this use, the word "well" will describe a noun or pronoun.

    You are very *well* today.

As an adverb, the word "well" describes an action done with skill or in a proper way. In this use, it will describe a verb.

    Ben writes very *well*.

"Real" and "Really." "Real" is an adjective that you use to describe something as authentic. "Really" is an adverb, or intensifier, used to emphasize an adjective or another adverb.

    Incorrect: Habib is real friendly.
    Correct: Habib is *really* friendly.
                   Habib is a *real* friend.

The Double Negative. The words we use to show negative are "no," "not," "none," "nothing," "never," "nobody," and the contraction "n't." Use only one of these words in any sentence.

    Incorrect: It didn't do no harm.
    Correct: It *didn't* do any harm.
                   It *did no* harm.
    Incorrect: Nobody saw nothing.
    Correct: *Nobody* saw anything.

Notice that when the contraction "n't" is used for "not," the contraction becomes part of the verb: could not/couldn't; have not/haven't; were not/weren't.

Some other words are also negative: hardly, scarcely, barely. Do not use them with negatives. Problems with these words often occur in contractions.

    Incorrect: Jamie couldn't hardly lift the weight.
    Correct: Jamie *could hardly* lift the weight.

USE MODIFIERS AND NEGATIVES CORRECTLY

Circle the correct word of the two given in parentheses. Write the part of speech of the word you select.

1. The plan sounded (good, well). _____
2. The band played (good, well). _____
3. The formation seems (good, well). _____
4. Jeff didn't hear (any, no) whistle. _____
5. Nothing (could, couldn't) stop our team. _____
6. Nghi (could, couldn't) hardly stop cheering. _____
7. Please don't tell me (any, no) excuses. _____
8. Our passing game goes (good, well) with our running game. _____
9. Our offense and defense look (good, well) together. _____
10. We hadn't heard (anything, nothing) from the coach. _____
11. There (are, aren't) no teams that can beat us. _____
12. The principal hasn't told (anybody, nobody) about the championship. _____
13. Dean is so excited he (can, can't) hardly breathe. _____
14. Gino wasn't (ever, never) on a winning team before. _____
15. Stephanie has (ever, never) been a happier cheerleader. _____

We hope you have noticed how much easier it is to explain these points now that you can identify the parts of speech. One of the main goals of this book is to give you a vocabulary to talk about your writing. Therefore, you should try to describe your reasons for the choices you make in grammar. Putting ideas into words often makes them clearer in our own minds.

> Check over some of your recent writing. Have you misused "good" or "well"? Have you used a double negative? If so, write the correct words and sentences, if you have not already done so. You will learn much more by correcting the mistakes you actually make than you will by doing the exercises in this book.

PART ONE: THE PARTS OF SPEECH   49

REVIEW: USING MODIFIERS

Identify adjectives and adverbs

Write whether each italicized word is an adjective or an adverb. Then circle the word and draw a line to the word it modifies.

1. *Suddenly* the lights went out. _____

2. A *cold*, _____

    damp wind swept through the room. _____

3. We were *too terrified* to speak. _____

4. A *dim* light _____

    gradually appeared _____

    near the ceiling. _____

5. Then an *extremely* _____

    soft voice began to whisper. _____

6. The *barely* _____

    audible words were in a _____

    strange language. _____

7. The *front* door was our _____

    only escape. _____

8. With *shaking* legs we inched _____

    our way *backwards*. _____

> Use the ideas above to write a mystery story. Use only the modifiers that create the effect you want. Too many modifiers can ruin a story.

Use modifiers correctly

Circle the correct word for each sentence.
1. Stephen Leacock may be Canada's (more, most) famous writer.
2. His books and stories are (funnier, funniest) than many written today.
3. He wrote his (better, best) work early in the twentieth century.
4. He liked to laugh at things other people took (serious, seriously).

5. Leacock was a (simple, simply) plain man.
6. His neighbours didn't mind (none, any) of his stories.
7. His (better, best) known book is *Sunshine Sketches of a Little Town*.
8. His books were (very, real) popular for many years.
9. Leacock wrote (amusingly, amusing) stories about the (more, most) ordinary events.
10. Haven't you (ever, never) been embarrassed?
11. Leacock's story about a (nervous, nervously) man in a bank is famous.
12. He wrote (good, well) about things he knew.
13. His witty satires on mystery stories are (real, really) wonderful.
14. One of his stories is about a (poor, poorer) swimming coach who couldn't swim.
15. (Sudden, Suddenly) the man fell into the pool.
16. One of his students (alert, alertly) rescued him.
17. The man was (prompt, promptly) fired.
18. His (former, formerly) students taught him how to swim.
19. (Lucky, Luckily) the coach got a job at another school.
20. Almost (immediate, immediately) he was fired again.
21. The (angry, angrily) new principal found the man couldn't teach.
22. The man got several other jobs with the same (unhappy, unhappily) result.
23. He now (supposed, supposedly) teaches people to fly.

> Find some books by Stephen Leacock in your school or local library. Most of his stories are quite short. Browse through the books, reading the stories that interest you. Here are some short story titles to look for: *My Financial Career*; *Buggam Grange: A Good Old Ghost Story*; *How We Kept Mother's Day*; *Simple Stories of Success or How To Succeed in Life*; *The New Food*.

PREPOSITIONS

Prepositions are connecting words. They connect one word or group of words to another. We have already used prepositions in this workbook, and you use them in almost every sentence you speak. Now we will learn to identify them and to see how they are used.

Prepositions show how two ideas are related in time, space, or in some other way. A preposition is placed before a noun (and its modifiers) or a pronoun to show its relationship to another word.

PART ONE: THE PARTS OF SPEECH

Here are some common prepositions:
Showing relationships in space: to, from, through, around, past, into, in, towards, with, without, above, below, beside, near, under, on
Showing relationships in time: before, after, during, until

One large group of prepositions shows a relationship of space. Think of holding this book in one hand and a pencil in the other. Now think of all the places the pencil could be in relation to the book. The pencil could be *above, below, beside,* or *on* the book. You could move it *to* or *from* the book. These short words are all prepositions. There are many others.

Another large group of prepositions shows a relationship of time. Think about when you did the activity with the pencil and the book in relation to some other time. You would use words such as "before," "after," "during," "while."
    I did this *before* lunch.   I did this *after* the bell rang.
    I did this *during* class.   I did this *while* I walked.

Other prepositions, such as "about," "for," "like," "from," or "with," show other kinds of relationships. There are far too many prepositions to list them all here. You know most of them already. Some students find it helpful to think of the "position" part of the word "preposition" as showing an idea's position in time or space.

Prepositions begin **prepositional phrases**. A prepositional phrase consists of a preposition, a noun or pronoun, and any modifiers of the noun. The noun or pronoun is called the object of the preposition.
Examples:
    from the school   by the red car   after three more years

FIND THE PREPOSITIONAL PHRASES

Underline the prepositional phrases. Circle the preposition and draw a line from the preposition to its object.
1. The thief slipped into the room.
2. The safe was hidden behind the picture.
3. It was a race against time.
4. Near the floor was an electric eye.
5. It was connected to an alarm system.
6. The thief had some gadgets in her pocket.
7. She shone an ultraviolet light around the room.
8. The purple beam of light showed the location of the electric eye.
9. She carefully stepped over it.
10. For thirty seconds, she stood motionless.

11. Without a sound, she moved toward the picture.//
12. In the safe were cash and bonds worth millions of dollars.
13. Everything was under control except the time.
14. She heard voices from upstairs.
15. The residents were supposed to be gone from the house.
16. Soon the house was again in silence.
17. She knew the combination to the safe.
18. Could she open it before the time limit?

> Finish the story suggested by the sentences above. Then look back at the story you wrote yourself and find some prepositional phrases that you used.

PREPOSITIONAL PHRASES AS MODIFIERS

Some prepositional phrases modify nouns. These phrases often tell *which one* or *what kind* about the noun. Because these phrases are used as adjectives, they are called **adjective phrases**.

   The desk *in the corner* is mine.
   ("In the corner" is an adjective phrase modifying the noun "desk." The preposition is "in" and the object of the preposition is "corner.")

   Some *of the players* were injured.
   ("Of the players" is an adjective phrase modifying the pronoun "some." The preposition is "of" and the object of the preposition is "players.")

Some prepositional phrases modify verbs. These phrases often tell *how, when, where*, or *to what extent* about the verb. Because these phrases are used as adverbs, they are called **adverb phrases**.

   We worked *without a break*.
   ("Without a break" is an adverb phrase modifying the verb "worked." The preposition is "without" and the object of the preposition is "break.")
   In June, Mrs. Lee will retire.
   ("In June" is an adverb phrase modifying the verb "will retire." The preposition is "in" and the object of the preposition is "June.")

Identify the prepositional phrases

Underline the prepositional phrases. Circle the word the phrase modifies. Then write "adjective" or "adverb" to tell what kind of prepositional phrase it is.

1. Dolphins live in the sea. _____

2. Some of these animals seem to communicate
   with humans. _____

PART ONE: THE PARTS OF SPEECH 53

3. They often swim near humans. _____

4. Squeaking noises come from their throats. _____

5. Scientists in boats have recorded the sounds. _____

6. They analyze the sounds at great length. _____

7. Dolphins in captivity become very friendly. _____

8. Many shows at water parks feature dolphins. _____

9. The lines of their mouths look like smiles. _____

10. Dolphins seem to speak to each other. _____

11. Dolphins in groups make many different sounds. _____

12. They play games with each other. _____

13. Biologists at some universities say dolphins have high intelligence. _____

14. The learning capacity of dolphins is greater than that of dogs or horses. _____

15. Some scientists argue that it is not possible to compare the intelligence of different species. _____

16. The controversy about this matter is unsettled. _____

17. Killer whales are in the same category. _____

18. How could you distinguish between two different species? _____

19. How could you compare an elephant's intelligence with a horse's intelligence? _____

20. The debate on this matter continues. _____

Do you think humans could ever learn to communicate with animals? Many people seem to communicate with their pets. Could this be called language? Studies have been done with chimpanzees that seem to show they can learn human language. You might like to look up some of this research and write something on the topic.

PREPOSITION OR ADVERB?

Many words used as prepositions may also be used as adverbs. How can you tell the difference? A preposition is never used alone. A preposition begins a prepositional phrase and will be followed by a noun or pronoun.

  The child went *inside the house.* Gordon looked *out the window.*

If the word is not followed by a noun or pronoun, it is probably an adverb.

  The child went inside. Gordon looked out.

Identify the prepositions and adverbs

Write whether the italicized word is a preposition or an adverb. If it is a preposition, circle its object.

1. The stage lights finally went *on*.   _____
2. The spotlight was focused *on* the singer.   _____
3. One fan fell *down* in a faint.   _____
4. The star walked *down* the stage   _____

   toward the audience.   _____
5. The backup group came *across* the stage.   _____
6. Their vocals just did not come *across* well.   _____
7. Our friends walked *along* the aisles.   _____
8. Julie did not come *along* tonight.   _____
9. The smoke made it hard to see *past* the front row.   _____
10. Some men with fans trotted *past*.   _____
11. The whole program was running *behind* schedule.   _____
12. Any stragglers were left *behind*.   _____
13. The comics went *through* their whole routine.   _____
14. Our plans to perform fell *through* at the last minute.   _____
15. The managers turned the volume *down*   _____

    after a few numbers.   _____

16. Angie pulled the hood *of* _____

    her jacket *up*. _____

17. *Down* the drain went dreams of stardom. _____

18. *On* the left were the trailers _____

    of the performers. _____

19. *Over* the loudspeakers came loud static. _____

20. The stage lights were left *on* _____

    after the finale. _____

Some linguists (people who study language) prefer to call these short adverbs part of the verb. For example, rather than say "give" is a verb and "up" is an adverb, they would say the verb is "give up." Here are some other verbs that could be considered in the same way: get along with, bring up, go back, think of, come back, take out, come to, put off, take up, take off, run into.

As an example of how these words might be confused with prepositions, consider these sentences.

    Bringing the chair up the stairs was difficult.
    Bringing children up the right way is difficult.
    The troublemaker was *put off* the team.
    Ted *put off* doing his essay.
    Please *come* to my party.
    He did not *come to* until the next day.

Think of some other sentences like these. Discuss your opinions on whether these words should be considered adverbs or as parts of the verb. When your class comes to a decision, use that method of describing these words.

CONJUNCTIONS

Conjunctions are another type of connecting word. Conjunctions are the words that join the parts of a compound together. The most common conjunctions are "and," "but," and "or."

Dina *and* Mel prepared the slide show.	(two proper nouns)
The paint cracked *and* peeled.	(two verbs)
His speech was short *but* interesting.	(two adjectives)
You can use chocolate *or* carob.	(two nouns)
Ask Jean *or* Rena for the answer.	(two proper nouns)
The gift is from Amanda *and* me.	(proper noun and pronoun)

Some conjunctions are used in pairs. Because they relate to each other, they are called **correlative conjunctions**. Here are some of the most common correlative conjunctions.

Both the manager *and* her assistant were in the store.
Either Nadia *or* Robin will meet you.
Neither Michael *nor* Sheila had enough money.
The machine *not only* copies material *but* also sorts it.
I didn't know *whether* to speak *or* not.

Recognize conjunctions

Circle the conjunctions in these sentences. Underline the words that are joined by the conjunctions.

1. Greg enjoys basketball and track.
2. Does he like hockey or soccer?
3. Both football and basketball are popular sports.
4. Cam entered the race but did not finish.
5. Neither the coach nor his friends knew what happened.
6. He groaned and grasped his ankle.
7. Do you think he will miss a race or two?
8. Lisa not only won the race but also broke the record.
9. She described her feat proudly but quietly.
10. The questioners were newspaper and TV reporters.
11. You can't win or lose unless you compete.
12. Victory and defeat are both good teachers.
13. The women's hockey team practised hard but carefully.
14. The TV report mentioned both the winners and the losers.
15. Can you upgrade or replace our equipment?

REVIEW: USING PREPOSITIONS AND CONJUNCTIONS

Identify the prepositional phrases

Circle each prepositional phrase. Write whether each is used as an adjective phrase or as an adverb phrase.

1. A snake is an animal with a long, legless body. _____

2. The body is covered by scales. _____

3. A snake usually slides on its belly. _____

4. The eyes are covered by scales and not by moveable eyelids. _____

Part One: The Parts of Speech   57

5. A snake's tongue brings odours to a sense organ in its mouth. _____

6. Snakes are members of the group called reptiles. _____

7. They probably developed from lizards millions of years ago. _____

8. Only a few countries in the world have no snakes. _____

9. Cobra snakes have poor vision in bright light. _____

10. Cobras are most active during the rainy season. _____

11. Cobras strike by rising half of their length then falling forward. _____

12. They must be fairly close to their victim. _____

Recognize conjunctions

Circle the conjunctions used in these sentences. Underline the two words or groups of words that are joined by each conjunction.

1. Boa constrictors are found in rain forests and semi-deserts.
2. They may be found either in trees or on the ground.
3. Boas are dangerous to humans but are not poisonous.
4. They use both their teeth and their body to attack prey.
5. Boa constrictors suffocate their prey by coiling their bodies around it and squeezing.
6. The victim is seldom crushed or deformed by the pressure.
7. Loss of habitat, the trade in skins, and the pet trade are the main threats to boa constrictors.
8. Canada's snakes are much smaller and less dangerous than those in the tropics.
9. The massasauga rattlesnake is sometimes found near cottages or lakes.
10. Snakes are both feared and hated by many people.
11. Many snakes offer both benefits and assistance to humans.
12. Some people want to neither hear nor read about snakes.

Snakes are a good topic for research. See if you can find ways in which snakes are helpful to humans. Why do you think so many people dislike snakes?

THE PARTS OF SPEECH

You have now learned the names of seven different kinds of words.

    nouns   verbs   adverbs   conjunctions
    pronouns   adjectives   prepositions

You also learned about noun markers (the articles "a," "an," and "the"), possessive pronouns, and possessive adjectives.

There is one other part of speech that we have not yet studied. An **interjection** is a word or group of words used to express strong feeling.

    Oh, no! Not another part of speech.   *Wow!* Did you see that?

This makes eight parts of speech that you know, plus noun markers.

IDENTIFY THE PARTS OF SPEECH

Write the part of speech of each italicized word.

1. The Princess of Amen-Ra *lived* in Egypt about 1500 BCE. _____

2. When *she* died, her body was laid in an _____

   ornate tomb deep in a vault at Luxor. _____

3. *During* excavations in the _____

   late 1890s, an Englishman _____

   bought the mummy case. _____

4. He *took* the case to _____

   his hotel, went for a walk _____

   and was never seen again. _____

5. He was travelling *with* _____

   three other men. _____

6. One of *them* was accidentally shot, _____

   another *lost* all his money in a bank failure, _____

   and the fourth became *severely* ill. _____

7. The coffin *reached* England and was bought by a businessman. _____

8. *Soon* three of his family were injured in a car _____

   accident and his *house* was damaged by fire. _____

PART ONE: THE PARTS OF SPEECH   59

9. He *gave* the coffin to the British Museum. _____

10. When *it* was being unloaded _____

    one workman fell and broke his leg. _____

11. A few days later the man helping him *suddenly* died. _____

12. When the Princess was put *on* display _____

    in the museum, *strange* noises _____

    and sobbing were heard from the coffin. _____

13. *Several* cleaners and other workers had _____

    frightening experiences near the coffin. _____

14. *Finally*, the mummy case was put _____

    into the basement. _____

15. Within *a* week, one of the two workers _____

    who carried *it* was seriously ill. _____

16. The *supervisor* of the move was _____

    found *dead* at his desk. _____

17. By now the *mummy's* case _____

    was *famous*. _____

18. A photographer *took a picture* of the coffin. _____

19. After developing the picture, *he* shot himself. _____

20. *Misfortune* continued to strike _____

    anyone who had contact with it. _____

21. *No* other museum in _____

    Britain would handle it. _____

22. Finally, an *American* archaeologist _____

    bought it _____

    and arranged to have it shipped. _____

23. *In April*, 1912, the _____

    new owner accompanied his _____

    treasure aboard the ship to America. _____

24. The ship was the *Titanic*. _____

> Creepy? Can you find out more information about this case? It's an interesting topic to research. It might also suggest a mystery story or a description.

WORDS USED IN DIFFERENT WAYS

There is only one way to be sure what part of speech a word is. That is to decide how the word is being used in a particular sentence. The same word can be used as several different parts of speech.

Somebody called the *police*.	(noun)
They arrived with a *police* dog.	(adjective)
They *police* this area every night.	(verb)
I usually watch TV as I *iron*.	(verb)
The heavy bar is made of *iron*.	(noun)
The magnet attracts *iron* filings.	(adjective)

A good test of your knowledge of the parts of speech is to see if you can tell the difference between two uses of the same word.

Determining the parts of speech

Decide what part of speech the italicized word is. Write your answer.

1. *That* watch looks expensive. _____

2. *That* is a mistake. _____

3. A stranger *left* the watch on a park bench. _____

4. The bench is on the *left* side of the path. _____

5. A strange *echo* was heard in the hallway. _____

6. The corridor became a huge *echo* chamber. _____

7. *Today* is my lucky day. _____

8. We are leaving *today* on an excursion. _____

9. The sunscreen should *block* the harmful rays. _____

PART ONE: THE PARTS OF SPEECH

10. Let's take a walk around the *block*. _____
11. I asked the vendor to *change* a ten-dollar bill. _____
12. I paid for the drinks and counted my *change*. _____
13. It was almost time for our *flight*. _____
14. We bought *flight* insurance before boarding. _____
15. Would you like to go *out* tonight? _____
16. The handlers threw our luggage *out* the window. _____
17. Are you sure you can *handle* this task? _____
18. I broke the *handle* on my suitcase. _____

REVIEW: THE PARTS OF SPEECH

IDENTIFY THE PARTS OF SPEECH

Write the part of speech of each italicized word.

1. The ship was three *football* fields in length and eleven stories high. _____
2. It was a gigantic *luxury* ship. _____
3. The name of the ship was *Titanic*. _____
4. Newspapers *around* the world _____

   reported on its first voyage. _____
5. *Hundreds* of the _____

   wealthiest people in the world _____

   were *aboard*. _____
6. The famous ship was the most *advanced* _____

   and the safest *liner* ever built. _____
7. The captain *maintained* speed and a _____

   northerly course *through* the ice fields. _____
8. *His* goal was to reach New York in _____

   record time. _____

9. Just before midnight, a lookout *spotted* an iceberg.

10. *At first* the great ship seemed to have avoided the *ice*.

11. *Underwater*, the iceberg tore a gash out of the side of the ship.

12. Most *passengers* thought it was just a bump.

13. *Within* minutes compartments were flooded.

14. There were not *enough* lifeboats for all the people aboard.

15. Women *and* children were put in lifeboats *first*.

16. The band *tried* to keep people *calm* *by* playing lively music.

17. *Soon* the ship was listing *badly*.

18. Some lifeboats were leaving *half* full.

19. Other lifeboats were *overcrowded* and in danger of capsizing.

20. People *leaped into* the *frigid* waters and drowned.

21. More than *1500* people were killed.

22. The *unsinkable* ship had sailed for a little more than four days.

23. Several *very* popular movies have been made about the *ship's* voyage.

24. Many questions are *still* unanswered.

PART ONE: THE PARTS OF SPEECH　　　　　　　　　　　　　　　63

25. *Some* artifacts have been recovered　　　　_____

    from the wreckage.　　　　　　　　　　　　_____

26. The ship *remains* in its　　　　　　　　　　_____

    underwater grave.　　　　　　　　　　　　_____

The 1998 movie, *Titanic*, contained some interesting footage of the wreckage. When was the wreckage of the *Titanic* found? The search for the wreck of the *Titanic* is another great story. There are also many other fascinating stories—some true, some unproved. You might like to do some research on the *Titanic* and write about some lesser-known facts about it.

PART TWO

The Sentence

Simple Subjects and Predicates 66	Review: Using Complete Sentences 98
Finding the Subject and the Predicate 67	Compound Constructions 100
Agreement in Number 69	Compound Subjects and Verb Agreements 102
Agreements to Watch For 70	Simple Sentences 103
Review: Making Subjects and Verbs Agree 71	Compound Sentences 104
When the Subject Does Not Come First 72	Punctuating Compound Sentences 107
Nouns Used as Subjects 74	The Subordinate Clause 109
Pronouns Used as Subjects 76	The Complex Sentence 112
Direct Objects 77	Noun Clauses 113
Indirect Objects 78	Adverb Clauses 115
Review: How Nouns Are Used in Sentences 79	Adjective Clauses 117
Object Form of Pronouns 81	Review: Subordinate Clauses 119
Transitive and Intransitive Verbs 82	Variety in Sentence Beginnings 121
Subjective Completions 83	Compound–Complex Sentences . . 123
Predicate Nouns 85	Review: Using Compound and Complex Sentences 125
Predicate Adjectives 86	The Last Word 127
Direct Object or Subjective Completion? 88	
Pronouns as Subjective Completions 89	
Compound Parts in a Sentence 92	
Review: The Sentence and Its Parts . . 93	
Kinds of Sentences 95	
Sentence Fragments 96	

IRWIN GRAMMAR SKILLS

SIMPLE SUBJECTS AND PREDICATES

There are two key words in a sentence: the **noun** that tells what we are talking about, and the **verb** or action word that tells us something about that noun. They are like the skeleton or the building blocks of the sentence. The rest of the words complete the sentence.
Example:
> The girl sang.

We can easily see that we are talking about *the girl* and we are told that she *sang*. Not many sentences are that simple, but you can find the building blocks of longer sentences by looking for the **key noun** and **key verb**.
Example:
> The shy, dark-haired girl in the flowered dress sang beautifully in a soft, clear voice.

The basic sentence is still, "The girl sang." The words, "shy," "dark-haired," "in the flowered dress" describe the noun "girl." The words "beautifully in a soft, clear voice" describe the verb "sang."

The **complete subject** is the key noun and all the words related to it:
> *The dark-haired girl in the flowered dress*
> The key noun, "girl," is called the **simple subject**.

The **complete predicate** is the key verb and all the words related to it:
> *sang beautifully in a soft, clear voice*
> The key verb, "sang," is called the **simple predicate**.

The easiest way to find the simple subject is to find the simple predicate or the main verb in the sentence. Then ask yourself *Who?* or *What?* about the verb. The answer will be the simple subject.
> The decorators painted the house.
> The verb is "painted." Who painted? The decorators. "Decorators" is the simple subject.

Identify simple subjects and simple predicates

Underline the simple subject in each sentence once and the simple predicate (the verb) twice.
1. People wear hats.
2. Some hats keep the wearer from getting sunburn.
3. Mexicans call their wide hats sombreros.
4. Hard hats protect workers in many industries from injury.
5. In some countries, hats show social status.
6. Most of the time, a person uses a hat as part of a costume.
7. Some schools forbid wearing hats indoors.
8. Many students believe that hats have no effect on learning.

PART TWO: THE SENTENCE

9. Some parents argue that wearing a hat inside shows bad manners.
10. Tastes in hats change with the times.
11. Very few men own a top hat these days.
12. People rent formal clothing when they need it.
13. Most women gave away their old hats long ago.
14. Movies often cause changes in style.
15. Fans imitate the style of the movie star.
16. Designers create new fashions in the style of the movie.
17. Many young people plan a career in fashion design.

FINDING THE SUBJECT AND THE PREDICATE

Being able to find the subject and the predicate in a sentence is helpful in reading as well as in writing. Have you ever been puzzled by something you're reading? Maybe you asked yourself, "What is this about?" You were really asking, "What is the subject of this sentence?" When we write, we sometimes get excited about what we are saying and forget to give our readers enough information to understand us. This happens most often when we are writing long sentences. This exercise will give you some practice with short sentences. Later in the book we will work with longer ones.

The **subject** usually contains a noun and all the words that modify that noun. Sometimes there is no noun, but a pronoun takes its place.
Example:
    Sharks eat. (no problem)
    Great white sharks, the fiercest creatures in the sea, eat almost anything they can get their teeth into.
    The subject is "sharks" and all the words that modify "sharks" (Great white, the fiercest creatures in the sea).
    It is a terrifying creature. (The subject is the pronoun "it." Pronouns are not modified, so there are no other words in the subject.)

The **predicate** contains a verb and all the words that modify that verb. In the sample above, the verb is "eat" and the related words tell us what they eat (almost anything they can get their teeth into).
To summarize:
    Subject: who or what the sentence is about
                    (a noun and its modifiers or a pronoun)
    Predicate: what is said about the subject
                    (a verb and its modifiers)

Identify subject and predicate

Draw a vertical line between the subject and the predicate in each sentence below. Be careful. Three of the items are not complete sentences. When you find these, write "subject" if it contains only a subject; write "predicate" if it contains only a predicate.

1. Some people believe in the Abominable Snowman.
2. The large, hairy creatures live in the Himalayan Mountains.
3. People in other parts of the world have seen similar creatures.
4. Canadians call their creature the Sasquatch.
5. Walks upright on two legs and bent over like an ape.
6. Some hunters took pictures of the Sasquatch a few years ago.
7. The pictures showed a human-like creature with long hair and long dangling arms.
8. Avoids human contact by running away.
9. Many other people think the story is a hoax.
10. The photos, which were out of focus and grainy.
11. Enlargements and photo enhancement seemed to prove it was real.
12. Some mountain climbers found huge footprints.
13. The prints were made by bears and then melted into larger forms.
14. A critic studied a photo of Sasquatch.
15. He identified a belt buckle hanging down from the animal's side.
16. Many people now believe that sasquatch is a phony.
17. The Himalayan creature may be real.

> Look at some sentences from a piece of your own writing. Draw a line between the subject and the predicate in each sentence.

AGREEMENT IN NUMBER

The word "agreement," from the root word "agree," has many meanings. In this exercise, it means "matching." The number of a word refers to whether it is singular or plural. You know that nouns change in form to show a change in number. A singular noun refers to one thing; a plural noun refers to more than one thing.

    girl/girls   woman/women   city/cities

The verb that tells something about the noun also changes.
    The girl goes to our school.   The girls go to our school.
    The city is in Saskatchewan.   The cities are in Saskatchewan.

A singular subject must have a singular verb form. A plural subject must have a plural verb form. When the subject and the verb match, they are said to agree in number.

Errors sometimes are found when a phrase comes between the subject and the verb.
    That pile of books is mine.
    (The subject, "pile," is singular, so the verb form is also singular.)
    Two boxes of food are empty.
    (The subject, "boxes," is plural, so the verb is also plural.)
    The videos on this shelf are not for sale.
    (The subject, "videos," is plural so the plural verb form, "are," is used.)
    The writer of all those great songs is unknown.
    (The subject, "writer," is singular, so the singular verb form, "is," is used.)

The subject of a verb is never found in a prepositional phrase. If you have learned how to identify verbs and their subjects, you should not make this mistake. The problem usually arises when we are in a hurry and we forget which word is the subject. Rereading your work will point out any mistakes.

Sometimes a phrase seems to make the subject plural because we seem to be talking about more than one thing.
    The coach, together with the players, is in the gym.
    The uniforms, along with the equipment, are new.

Some other prepositions like these are: "with," "including," "as well as," "in addition to."

Notice that these phrases modify the noun. The noun is the subject and the verb must agree with it in number. Using "and," however, creates a compound subject, which we will discuss later, and the plural form of the verb is used.
    Leah and Tracy are at the movies.

MAKE THE SUBJECT AND THE VERB AGREE

Circle the correct form of the verb.
1. The evidence (has, have) been turned in.
2. The items on the desk (is, are) from the scene of the crime.
3. The questioning by the officers (has, have) been completed.
4. Information about the events (has, have) been gathered.
5. One suspect among the men (has, have) been charged.
6. One woman, along with her friends, (is, are) still a suspect.
7. The report, including the fingerprints, (show, shows) what happened.
8. The footprints at the scene (is, are) quite clear.
9. The two men (was, were) nearby at the time.
10. The question of two arrests (was, were) discussed.
11. Each man (claims, claim) to be the most honest.
12. The clothes on the victim (was, were) dirty and torn.
13. Three of the suspects (has, have) been in custody before.
14. The review board (meet, meets) each morning.
15. The lawyer for the suspects (feel, feels) quite angry.
16. The crime, along with its effect, (is, are) very unusual.
17. The victim's wallet, along with his car keys, (was, were) not taken.
18. Crimes of this kind (is, are) rarely seen.

> The sentences above suggest some clues to a crime. What was the crime? Write a story suggested by the sentences in this exercise.

AGREEMENTS TO WATCH FOR

"Doesn't" and "Don't." Problems sometimes occur when "doesn't" and "don't" are used with pronouns. "Doesn't" is used with the subjects "he," "she," and "it." "Don't" is used with all other pronouns.

  It *doesn't* make sense. She *doesn't* care. He *doesn't* want to go.
  They *don't* like baking. We *don't* agree. I *don't* listen.

Sentences beginning with "there," "here," or "where." When one of these words begins a sentence, the subject comes after the verb. Use the verb that agrees with the subject.

  There is no harm in this. *There* are six empty seats.
  Here is the book you wanted. *Here* are the lab notes.
  Where is Zackery? *Where* are the others?

PART TWO: THE SENTENCE

MAKE THE SUBJECTS AND VERBS AGREE

Circle the correct form of the verb. Underline the subject of the verb.
1. Here (is, are) the magazines you wanted.
2. (Doesn't, Don't) he want them anymore?
3. Where (is, are) the indexes?
4. There (seem, seems) to be something missing.
5. It (doesn't, don't) boot up.
6. Here (come, comes) the teacher now.
7. There (is, are) three possible causes for this.
8. There (go, goes) the bell.
9. (Doesn't, Don't) you care about my problem?
10. Where (is, are) Nicola and Manny?
11. She (doesn't, don't) have a computer at home.
12. There (appear, appears) to be a power failure.
13. Here (is, are) my plan.
14. Danny (doesn't, don't) use his computer much.
15. (Doesn't, Don't) his sisters use it?
16. Where (was, were) the floppy disks?
17. There (is, are) supposed to be two boxes of them.
18. (Is, Are) there any disks left?
19. Angie (doesn't, don't) know what happened to them.
20. The technician (doesn't, don't) know what the problem is.

REVIEW: MAKING SUBJECTS AND VERBS AGREE

MAKE THE SUBJECTS AND VERBS AGREE

Circle the correct verb. Underline its subject.
1. The movie about skin divers (was, were) really interesting.
2. All of the divers (is, are) well trained.
3. Both the diver and the equipment (is, are) important.
4. Each of the dives (require, requires) careful planning.
5. There (is, are) many risks in diving.
6. Neither the diver nor the assistants in the boat (is, are) able to relax.
7. Either a breath-holding dive or scuba diving (is, are) exciting.
8. Where (is, are) the training school and the teacher?
9. Several of the divers (create, creates) their own diving gear.

10. (Don't, Doesn't) a diver need an assistant?
11. Neither of these types of diving (is, are) without danger.
12. Everyone involved (know, knows) what is at stake.
13. A new diver without a trained assistant (is, are) taking a big risk.
14. There (is, are) often unexpected problems.
15. Most of the danger (is, are) from inexperience.
16. It (doesn't, don't) help to panic underwater.
17. Here (come, comes) a shark!
18. Shell divers, along with people in search of food, (has, have) been famous for years.
19. The snorkel used by divers (has, have) been around for thousands of years.
20. Neither the snorkel nor goggles (is, are) new inventions.
21. The facemask with glass lenses (was, were) first used about one hundred years ago.
22. Jacques Cousteau, along with some others, (was, were) the inventor of the aqualung.
23. The first letters of the words "self-contained underwater breathing apparatus" (is, are) used to form the word "scuba."
24. None of the show divers (use, uses) any equipment.
25. Everything they do (is, are) by their own strength and ability.
26. The tourists, as well as the inhabitants, (marvel, marvels) at their skill.
27. (Doesn't, Don't) each of the divers risk his or her life?
28. The diver, together with her sponsors, (make, makes) a living during the tourist season.
29. (Is, Are) there any laws against this kind of diving?
30. How (is, are) the law and the police going to stop them?

WHEN THE SUBJECT DOES NOT COME FIRST

We have been working with short, simple sentences in which the subject has come before the verb. The sentences we have studied so far have all been **statements**. Some sentence structures, however, put the verb at the beginning. The most common structure where another part of the sentence comes first is in questions.

Example:
>Find the verb and the subject in each sentence. Remember that verbs might be made up of more than one word.
>Susanne scored the winning goal. (What is the verb? What is the subject?)

Did Susanne score the winning goal? (What is the verb? What is the subject?)

Another type of sentence is the **command**, and it is a little trickier. When you give a command or an order, it is quite clear whom you are addressing. Also, in a command the verb is the most important word; that is what you are ordering the person to do. So the verb comes first in a command. The subject often doesn't appear.
Examples:
Eat your cereal.
Change the channel.

Sometimes in a command the subject is added at the end after a comma.
Eat your cereal, *darling*.
Change the channel, *Charlie*.

It is also very common for a word or group of words to come before the subject.
The coach yelled at the team in a loud voice.
In a loud voice, the coach yelled at the team.

The key to these sentences is still to find the verb. Then ask yourself *Who?* or *What?* to find the subject. Use the time-change test if you are in doubt about the verb. In the example above, the verb is "yelled" and the subject is "coach," because the coach did the yelling.

A fourth sentence type where the subject does not come first uses introductory words such as "there" or "here." Again, find the verb and you will quickly find the subject.

FIND THE SUBJECTS THAT DO NOT COME FIRST

Circle the subject of each sentence. Underline the verb. If the sentence is a command, write "command."

1. Were the colonists murdered?
2. Did the people move to some other island?
3. There is a great mystery about the lost colony.
4. In 1587, a colony was established on Roanoke Island, Virginia.
5. Left on the island were more than one hundred people.
6. Make friends with the native people.
7. Did the people see smoke rising from the shore?
8. There was no one in the settlement.

9. Leave a sign if there is danger. _____

10. On a tree was carved the word "Croatoan." _____

11. Was the word meant as a message? _____

12. Fifty miles (80.5 km) to the south lay the island of Croatoan. _____

13. Afraid of bad weather, the rescuers did not go to the island. _____

14. Without the help of the native people, the settlers would not have lived. _____

15. There was no sign of struggle. _____

16. Today, the story remains a mystery. _____

> The topic of the sentences above is a true and interesting story. Use information in the exercise and research the lost colony of Roanoke, Virginia.

NOUNS USED AS SUBJECTS

In Part One of this book, you learned several things about nouns. Nouns:
- refer to a person, place, or thing
- show number (singular or plural)
- sometimes follow noun markers
- may be common or proper
- may be used as possessives

If you are not sure about some of these points, go back to Part One: The Parts of Speech, and review the work on nouns. We will now learn how nouns are used in sentences, so it is important that you can identify nouns. Here is a brief review of nouns.

IDENTIFY THE NOUNS

Underline the nouns. Circle the noun markers. Write "proper" after the sentence if it contains a proper noun. Note: Not all nouns have markers.

1. Fashion is a particular style. _____

2. The style may last for a few months or for many years. _____

PART TWO: THE SENTENCE   75

3. Cars, clothing, music, furniture, and art have fashions. _____

4. The most common fashions are in clothing. _____

5. Large hoop skirts were the fashion for women at one time. _____

6. Tall, round, dark hats were the fashion for men. _____

7. Music, dance, and clothing are often linked in a style. _____

8. Dior and Armani are famous names in modern fashion. _____

9. Clothing and fashion do not mean the same thing. _____

10. People follow fashions for many reasons. _____

Nouns are often used as the key word in the subject of the sentence, the word that tells what is being talked about in the sentence.

IDENTIFY NOUNS USED AS SUBJECTS

Underline only the nouns used as subjects in each sentence. Circle the noun markers in the subject, if there are any. A subject may have two or more nouns joined together. This is called a **compound subject**.

1. Some people want to imitate the style of wealthy or famous people.
2. Movies and television influence styles in dress.
3. Young people are often the first to adopt a fashion.
4. Their parents may disapprove of the style.
5. Blue jeans have been worn for over a hundred years.
6. Levi Strauss sold them first.
7. The styles of jeans have changed over the years.
8. Miners and farm workers wear them.
9. A modern teen wears jeans for different reasons.
10. The fashion industry has become a very large industry.

> What are your ideas about current fashions? You might like to write about your opinions.

PRONOUNS USED AS SUBJECTS

When a pronoun is the subject of a sentence, the **subject form** of the pronoun is used. The subject forms are:
    Singular: I, you, he, she, it
    Plural: we, you, they

You know how to find the subject of a sentence when it is a noun. Use the same method to find pronoun subjects. Find the verb, then find what pronoun the verb is telling something about.
    Vera made the decision. (The verb is "made"; it tells us what *Vera* did.)
    She made the decision. (The verb is "made"; it tells us what *she* did.)

USE THE SUBJECT FORM OF PRONOUNS

Circle the correct pronoun. If the verb is a linking verb, you might find it helpful to turn the sentence around, as we did in the example, to check your answer.

1. (We, Us) ordered a pizza.
2. The waiter was (he, him).
3. (They, Them) sat near us in the restaurant.
4. My friends are (they, them).
5. (He, Him) tripped over something.
6. It was (I, me) who saw what happened.
7. The most embarrassed person was (he, him).
8. (She, Her) helped him up.
9. The guilty ones were (they, them).
10. The owner of the restaurant was (he, him)
11. Was (he, him) the boss?
12. After a brief talk, (we, us) felt more calm.
13. Were the witnesses (they, them)?
14. Are (we, us) the only ones who saw what happened?
15. (He, Him) is the one you're looking for.
16. Is (she, her) still your friend?
17. The cleaner was (he, him).
18. (He, Him) thought it was a joke.
19. The sorry one was (he, him).

DIRECT OBJECTS

We have looked at sentences that contain a simple subject and a simple predicate (the verb). Here is a sample we used before.
    The girl sang.

The verb is "sang," which tells us what the girl did. The subject is the noun, "girl," which tells us who sang. But you might ask, "What did she sing?" We need to add another part to the sentence to tell you that.
    The girl sang a ballad.

What part of speech is "ballad"? The sentence now has another noun in the predicate. This part of the predicate is called the **direct object**.

The key to these sentences is still the verb. Find the verb and ask yourself *Who?* or *What?* and you can find the subject. Once you have found the subject and the verb, one way to find the direct object is to put them together and ask *Who?* or *What?* again. In the example, *The girl sang.* "What?" is answered by the words "a ballad." The word "ballad" is the direct object.

The direct object in a sentence will be a noun or a pronoun. Since you know how to identify nouns, you should have no trouble finding the direct objects in these sentences.

Find the direct objects

In each of these sentences, circle the verb. Then underline the direct object.
1. Galileo improved the telescope.
2. In school, he studied medicine at first.
3. The young man liked mathematics better.
4. In his time, people believed another theory.
5. The planets and the sun orbit the earth.
6. Galileo studied the heavens at night.
7. The careful observer discovered many new facts about the moon.
8. This astronomer also developed other theories.
9. Many people ridiculed the scientist.
10. His beliefs earned him many enemies.
11. The Church limited his teaching.
12. Galileo did not use the scientific method.
13. The original thinker reduced problems to simple terms.
14. His discoveries helped later scientists.
15. The USSR launched a satellite in 1957.
16. The United States sent larger spacecraft into the sky.

17. Humans reached the moon in 1969.
18. Neil Armstrong spoke some famous words.
19. Roberta Bondar orbited the earth.
20. Other Canadians have also visited outer space.

> Find some direct objects in the sentences that you have written recently. You will find that you know how to use direct objects. Now you also know what they are called. Having a vocabulary to talk about your writing will help you understand sentence structures and could help you become a better writer.

INDIRECT OBJECTS

Some sentences contain **indirect objects**. When we are speaking or writing, we often leave out words. Indirect objects are the result of leaving out prepositions—short words like "to," "for," "from," used to connect parts of a sentence.
Example:
>Jamal told his story to the coach.
>Jamal told the coach his story.

The two sentences have the same meaning. Notice three things with indirect objects:
>1) They are nouns (people, places, or things).
>2) They are shortened from phrases that begin with "to" or "for."
>3) They are placed before the direct object.

To find an indirect object, put the phrase back together in your head. Take the subject and the verb and ask *To what?* or *To whom?* If that doesn't work, ask *For whom?* or *For what?* If that doesn't work either, there is probably no indirect object in the sentence.
>Sal told the *director* his sad *story*. (There is both an indirect object and a direct object. We know *what* Sal told and *whom* he told it to.)
>Andrea bought *Tony* a *birthday cake*. (We know *what* Andrea bought and *whom* she bought it for.)

FIND THE INDIRECT OBJECT

In the sentences below, underline the indirect object and circle the verb.
1. The zoo offers students a discount.
2. The attendant sold Sonia a map.
3. Terri loaned Jim two dollars.
4. A guide showed the visitors the gorillas.
5. One ape handed the other a pail of sand.
6. Their antics gave the visitors a laugh.

PART TWO: THE SENTENCE   79

7. The restaurant sold the children soft drinks.
8. Their parents helped the smaller children find their lunches.
9. The older children bought their friends souvenirs.
10. The bus driver gave the passengers a comfortable ride.

DISTINGUISH BETWEEN DIRECT AND INDIRECT OBJECTS

Circle the verb in each sentence. State whether the word in italics is a direct object or an indirect object.

1. Nadia washed the *car*.   _____
2. Jerry offered *Trevor* ten dollars.   _____
3. The teacher gave the *class* a test.   _____
4. Matt ate a huge *meal* at lunchtime.   _____
5. Then he borrowed my science *notes*.   _____
6. Kaled gave his *friend* help with math.   _____
7. The science teacher gave Jesse a failing *grade*.   _____
8. Ramon will not believe *Trevor* again.   _____
9. Jamal told Nel a *lie*.   _____
10. The report card showed my *parents* what happened.   _____

> Indirect objects occur after only a few verbs. They occur more often in spoken language than in written language. As you are listening to a conversation today, see if you can identify the indirect objects that you hear.

REVIEW: HOW NOUNS ARE USED IN SENTENCES

One way to identify the direct object in a long sentence is to identify the verb (the simple predicate). Then find the noun that is the verb's subject. Read those two words together and ask *What?* or *Whom?* The answer usually shows you the direct object.

You should still use the noun markers and the number clue (singular or plural) to help identify the nouns.

Identify how nouns are used in sentences

You have three tasks in this exercise. First circle the nouns used as subjects; then underline the verbs; then circle the nouns used as direct objects. Be alert for compound nouns and verbs.

1. Teens have changed the economy.
2. Young people have more money than ever before.
3. Maybe you don't have enough money.
4. Advertisers aim their ads at teens.
5. Teenagers influence music, clothing and TV.
6. Each year, teens spend billions of dollars.
7. Young people use the Internet also.
8. Advertisers divide teens into two groups.
9. Children between nine and fourteen are called tweens.
10. Teens spend money to be like young adults.
11. A small percentage of teens gets money from jobs.
12. By the year 2004, teens will spend 4.4 million dollars.
13. Some companies join other companies for advertising.
14. Musicians and sports stars promote the products.
15. Young buyers purchase movies, toys, and clothing.
16. Concerts attract huge numbers of fans.
17. Companies pitch and sell clothing, records, and posters.
18. Many teens meet their friends at movie complexes.
19. Teenagers play video games.
20. Commercials bombard young people all day long.

What is your opinion on teen spending? Do you feel attacked by advertising? Can teens make their own decisions about what to buy? Do you think teens are influenced by other teens to buy things they might not want or need? Maybe you could write a composition on the topic.

OBJECT FORM OF PRONOUNS

When a personal pronoun is used as the direct object or as the indirect object, the **object form** is used. The object forms are:
- Singular: me, you, him, her, it
- Plural: us, you, them

The same rule applies when the pronoun is used as the object of a preposition. Examples:
My Dad plays golf with us. ("With" is a preposition; the object form of the pronoun, "us," is used after it.)
The teacher spoke to her. ("To" is a preposition; the object form, "her," is used after it.)

USE THE OBJECT FORM OF PRONOUNS

Circle the correct pronoun.
1. Did you forget (we, us)?
2. The long wait troubled (I, me).
3. Give the keys to (he, him).
4. The movie monster scared (they, them).
5. Julian loaned (we, us) some money.
6. The story is about (she, her).
7. Are you talking to (I, me)?
8. The manager asked (them, they) several questions.
9. Two tickets were for (she, her).
10. The subway gave (they, them) some shelter from the rain.
11. The conductor asked (he, him) to move along.
12. The raincoat belongs to (she, her).
13. The newspaper reporter wrote about (we, us).
14. The security guard showed (I, me) her badge.
15. The joke did not seem funny to (she, her).
16. Trouble always seems to find (he, him).
17. Was the ticket addressed to (she, her)?
18. Why did the judge question (I, me)?
19. Is the verdict fair to (he, him)?
20. Can you give (we, us) a ride home?

TRANSITIVE AND INTRANSITIVE VERBS

You learned how to identify verbs and the parts of verbs on pages 24–28. If you are not sure what verbs are, look back at those pages now. We said that verbs are words that show time. The time shown by a verb is called the **tense** of the verb.

Another helpful way to think about verbs is to find the action in a sentence. If a sentence talks about some action, the verb is the word that tells what the action is.
Examples:
>Rena painted the walls. (The action is painting and Rena performed that action. The verb is "painted.")

Verbs that are followed by a direct object are called **transitive verbs**. You know the word form "trans-" in words such as "transport," "transit," "transcend," etc. It means "across" or "over." A transitive verb tells that the action is carried over to the object.

In the example above, the subject is the noun, "Rena," the verb is "painted," and the direct object is "the walls." The verb "painted" is a transitive verb.

Not all sentences express an action. You already know about linking verbs. They just link the subject to a word in the predicate that describes or means the same as the subject.
>My brother is a banker.
>My brother is handsome.

Other sentences express an action but do not tell what was acted upon or what received the action.
>The dog growled.
>The dog growled fiercely. (The adverb "fiercely" describes the verb "growled." It does not tell that anything received the action.)

Action verbs that are not followed by a direct object are called **intransitive verbs**. An intransitive verb simply means that the verb is *not transitive*: the action is not carried to an object.

The same verb can be transitive in one sentence and intransitive in another.
>Pierre bounced the ball.
>The ball bounced.

PART TWO: THE SENTENCE

DISTINGUISH BETWEEN TRANSITIVE AND INTRANSITIVE VERBS

Underline the verb in each sentence. State whether it is transitive or intransitive.

1. The network cancelled the show. _____
2. The stars worked very hard. _____
3. The series ended suddenly. _____
4. The director took legal action. _____
5. A Canadian company produced the shows. _____
6. Large live audiences filled the studio. _____
7. The viewers protested. _____
8. Some people demonstrated outside the offices. _____
9. The cancellation disappointed many people. _____
10. My friends and I watched the show every week. _____
11. Letters of protest filled the mailroom. _____
12. New sponsors covered the costs. _____
13. Crew hands built a new set. _____
14. Viewers waited impatiently. _____
15. The revised show began the following season. _____

SUBJECTIVE COMPLETIONS

When a linking verb appears in a sentence, it links a word in the predicate to the key word in the subject (a noun or pronoun). These completing parts are called **subjective completions**. They mean the same as or modify the subject. For example:

My friend Nick is _____. (Whatever word we put in will tell us about the subject, "Nick," so the word will complete the subject.)

Our dog is a _____. (The completing word will tell us about the subject, "dog.")

The best singer is _____. (We could use a proper noun, such as a person's name, or we could use a pronoun, such as "he" or "she.")

Subjective completions may be nouns, adjectives, or pronouns.

As a check on identifying subjective completions, take the word you think might be a completion and put it with the subject. If the word could be used in the subject and still make sense, it is probably a completion. In the example sentences, we might use a word such as "clever" to describe Nick. We could also think of "clever Nick" and it would still make sense. In the second example, if we used the completion "spaniel," we could put it with the subject and read, "spaniel dog."

IDENTIFY THE SUBJECTIVE COMPLETIONS

Circle the linking verbs. Underline the subjective completions. State whether the completion is a noun or an adjective.

1. Dian Fossey was a biologist.
2. The young woman became interested in gorillas.
3. She felt sympathetic towards the great apes.
4. Fossey was a hero to many people.
5. At first, she seemed powerless to help them.
6. The small American was afraid of the huge animals.
7. Other people became worried about her.
8. Sometimes the gorillas seemed friendly to her.
9. Fossey was a very courageous woman.
10. Her friendships with the gorillas were the highlight of her life.
11. Loggers felt angry with her.
12. She appeared dangerous to them.
13. The movie about Dian Fossey is very interesting.
14. The author is the subject of that movie.
15. Dian Fossey became famous after the movie.

> You might like to find out more about Dian Fossey and her work with gorillas. Her story would make an interesting topic for an essay. The title of the movie about her is *Gorillas in the Mist*. A good book about apes is *Virunga*, by Farley Mowat.

PREDICATE NOUNS

When a noun is used as a subjective completion, it is called a **predicate noun**. Predicate nouns appear in the predicate of a sentence, after a linking verb. For example:

My best friend is Saeed. (The subject noun, "friend," and the subjective completion, "Saeed," both refer to the same person. "Saeed" is a predicate noun.)

That animal is a cheetah. (The subject noun, "animal," and the subjective completion, "cheetah," both refer to the same animal. "Cheetah" is a predicate noun.)

Not all nouns used in the predicate of a sentence are predicate nouns. Remember that direct and indirect objects may also be nouns. Your clue will be the verbs. Linking verbs are followed by subjective completions.

Identify nouns and predicate nouns

Underline the verbs in these sentences. Circle the nouns that are used as subjects. Then put a box around the nouns that are used as subjective completions; that is, the predicate nouns. Not every sentence in the exercise contains a predicate noun.

1. Nostradamus was a sixteenth-century visionary (a person who foretells the future).
2. At first, this seer predicted the weather.
3. A one-eyed man will be king.
4. The king was a fighting man.
5. The ruler lost an eye in a joust.
6. The prediction was true!
7. Nostradamus became famous.
8. Nostradamus was an intelligent man.
9. His predictions were puzzles.
10. The strange language was an invention.
11. Each prophecy was a four-line verse.
12. Many people today are believers.
13. His books are bestsellers throughout the world.
14. The year 2000 was a frightening time for some people.
15. The sayings of Nostradamus were a comfort to some.
16. Foretelling the future is a popular pastime.
17. Signs in the heavens may be symbols of the future.
18. Fortune-tellers and seers are often writers in newspapers.
19. Horoscopes are predictions about life.

> Can the future be foretold? Suppose we could know what is to happen. Would that be a good thing? Would there be problems with knowing the future? Foretelling the future is one aspect of ESP (extrasensory perception). Do you believe in ESP? Have you ever had an experience that you could not explain? You might like to do some research and write something about ESP, or find out more about Nostradamus and his predictions.

PREDICATE ADJECTIVES

When an adjective is used as a subjective completion, it is called a **predicate adjective**. A predicate adjective modifies the noun that is the subject of the sentence. For example,

> The cheetah is swift. (The adjective, "swift," describes the subject noun, "cheetah," but follows a linking verb in the predicate; "swift" is a predicate adjective.)
> That music is fantastic. (The adjective, "fantastic," modifies the subject noun, "music," but follows a linking verb; "fantastic" is a predicate adjective.)

Recognize predicate adjectives

Circle any predicate adjectives in the sentences below. For review and practice, underline any other type of adjectives you might find.

1. The American flamingo is tall and pinkish.
2. These creatures are colourful and graceful.
3. Their habitat is brackish, shallow water.
4. Flamingos are very sociable.
5. A flamingo's bill is long and useful.
6. Flamingos are popular and numerous.
7. Their chicks are tiny and helpless.
8. Young flamingos are vulnerable to large birds of prey.

Sometimes predicate adjectives are hard to distinguish from verbs. Earlier, you learned about the principal parts of a verb. If you are not clear on what that means, go back to page 30 and review them. Verb participles are often used as adjectives.

> The car has been stolen. ("Stolen" is the past participle of the verb "to steal.")
> That is a stolen car. (The adjective "stolen" modifies the noun "car.")

Another complication is the fact that forms of the verb "to be" (is, are, was, were) may be linking verbs or helping verbs. Linking verbs are followed by subjective completions. If the verb is a helping verb, there will be an action verb with it and there might be an object.

> The steel bar is bent. (The linking verb, "is," is followed by the predicate adjective, "bent.")
>
> The steel bar is bent in a huge machine. (The helping verb, "is," is used with the main verb, "bent," which suggests an action of bending. Someone or something bent the bar.)

How can you tell the difference? You must think about the meaning of the sentence. If the adjective in the predicate tells you about the condition or the state of the subject, then it is a predicate adjective (subjective completion). If the word suggests an action that was done to or by the subject, then it is probably a verb participle.

PRACTISE WITH PREDICATE ADJECTIVES

Here are some sentences for discussion. State the part of speech of each italicized word. State reasons for your decision.

1. The child was *lost* for two days.

2. The game was *lost* in the final minute.

3. The young athletes are very *agile*.

4. Amateur athletes are not *paid*.

5. The shirts were *stained* and *useless*.

6. The shirts were *stained* by the red dye.

7. The dresses were *ruined* after one day.

8. The dresses were *ruined* by the smoke.

9. The blade of the stick is *curved*.

   _____

10. The blade of the stick is *curved* in a vice.

    _____

DIRECT OBJECT OR SUBJECTIVE COMPLETION?

If a sentence contains a direct object, the noun in the predicate refers to something completely different from the noun in the subject.

If the sentence contains a subjective completion, the noun or pronoun in the predicate refers to the same thing or person as the noun in the subject. If the completion is an adjective, it will describe the noun in the subject.

Examples:
> *Simon* ate an *apple*. (The two nouns refer to two different things; "apple" is the direct object.)
> *Simon* is a *musician*. (The two nouns both refer to *Simon*; "musician" is a completion, a predicate noun.)
> Roch wrote an *exam*. ("Exam" is a direct object.)
> Roch is *tired*. ("Tired" is a completion, a predicate adjective.)

It might also help to remember that direct objects occur in sentences with action verbs. Subjective completions occur with non-action or linking verbs.

The exercise below contains some trick sentences. In some of them, we have used the same verb in two different sentences. In one case there will be a direct object; in the other there will be a subjective completion. This will test your understanding. It will also show how verbs can be used in different ways.

Direct object or subjective completion?

Find the difference between a direct object and a subjective completion. In each sentence, circle the verb. Then write whether the italicized word is a direct object or a subjective completion. Write "PN" if the completion is a predicate noun. Write "PA" if the completion is a predicate adjective.

1. My uncle grows *sleepy* in the evening.   _____

2. My uncle grows *potatoes* in the summer.   _____

3. Lonnie gets *angry* when you tease him.   _____

4. Lonnie gets top *marks* in every subject.   _____

PART TWO: THE SENTENCE   89

5. Randy ate three *hamburgers* for lunch.   _____

6. Randy was a *sick* boy all afternoon.   _____

7. The wicked witch sold the children a poisoned
    apple.   _____

8. The wicked witch was an *ugly* hag.   _____

9. Some students seem *confused* by these
    sentences.   _____

10. Jeremy felt *embarrassed* by his mistake.   _____

11. Jeremy felt the cold *metal* in his hand.   _____

12. At the party, we tasted Gina's *pizza*.   _____

13. Gina's pizza tasted *delicious*.   _____

14. Hillary will be our *pitcher* today.   _____

15. Hillary dropped the *pitcher* of water.   _____

> Look back at some sentences you have written recently. Find some direct objects and some subjective completions in your own sentences.

PRONOUNS AS SUBJECTIVE COMPLETIONS

When a pronoun is used as a subjective completion, the subject form is used. Remember that the completion is linked to the subject by a linking verb. The pronoun used as a completion refers to the subject or has the same meaning as the subject.

    The halfback is he. (There is a linking verb so both the noun, "halfback," and the pronoun, "he," refer to the same person.)

    If this sounds odd, turn the sentence around: *He is the halfback.*

    The subject forms of personal pronouns are: "I," "you," "he," "she," "it," "we," "they."

Here is another example.
    Question: Who rang the bell?
    Answer: The caller was I.
    (There is a linking verb, "was"; the pronoun, "I," refers to the noun "caller.")

This is a difficult point to remember, because in spoken language we often use the incorrect form.
Examples:
    Incorrect: That's him.   It's me.
    Correct: That is *he*.   It is *I*.

Notice that in question sentences, the verb comes first. You must then decide which word is the subject and which is the subjective completion.

IDENTIFY PRONOUNS USED AS SUBJECTIVE COMPLETIONS

Circle each pronoun that is used as a subjective completion. If the pronoun in a sentence is not used as a subjective completion, do not circle it.

1. Is she the team captain?
2. He was the captain last year.
3. It was they who saw the movie.
4. Am I your enemy?
5. The happiest camper was he.
6. Are those the only shoes you have?

USE THE CORRECT FORM

Circle the correct form of the pronoun for each sentence. State why you chose the form you did.

1. It was (I, me) who chose the music.
   _____

2. Give the present to (he, him).
   _____

3. Were (them, they) happy with the result?
   _____

4. That is (she, her).
   _____

5. The loudest singer in the group is (he, him).
   _____

6. Who thinks that (they, them) are the best?
   _____

The possessive forms of pronouns may also be used as subjective completions. Review possessive pronouns on page 14 if necessary. Some common possessive forms are "mine," "your," "his," "hers," "its," "our," "theirs."

The red locker is mine. (The possessive pronoun, "mine," is a subjective completion. "The locker" and "mine" refer to the same locker.)
The seats at the front are ours. (The possessive pronoun, "ours," is a subjective completion.)

These are not hard to identify if you think about the meaning of the sentence. Subjective completions tell about the subject, have the same meaning as the subject, or refer to the same thing that the subject refers to.

Identify the pronoun subjective completions

Circle the pronouns that are subjective completions in the sentences below. Correct any errors in form if necessary. State reasons for your decisions. Not all sentences contain a subjective completion.

1. The most popular exhibit was ours.

2. The first one finished was she.

3. After you pass a large green house, the next one on the left is mine.

4. How many candies have you eaten?

5. Was his the only application?

6. The person who called you last night was I.

7. We have finished our exercise and they will soon finish theirs.

8. The books on the table are hers.

COMPOUND PARTS IN A SENTENCE

A **compound** is something that is made up of two or more parts. In science class, you may mix substances to form a compound.

Any part of a sentence can be compound. Subjects, predicates, direct objects, indirect objects, and subjective completions can all have more than one part. You use compound parts of sentences in your speaking and writing all the time. This exercise will help you recognize them.

The words in a compound are joined by the words "or," "and," or "but" if there are two parts. If there are more than two parts, commas join the first parts and one of those words is used before the last part.
Examples:
      Curly, Larry, and Moe are the Three Stooges. (compound subject)
      The Three Stooges punch, kick, or gouge. (compound verb)
      They break furniture, windows, and lamps. (compound direct object)
      Curly offered Larry and Moe a birthday cake. (compound indirect object)
      They looked messy but happy. (compound subjective completion)

IDENTIFY COMPOUND SENTENCE PARTS

Circle the compound parts. Write whether they are subjects, verbs, objects, or subjective completions. (Did you notice the compound in the instruction?)

1. Crocodiles and alligators are very much alike. _____
2. They both are quiet, dangerous, and swift. _____
3. Their habitats are swamps, rivers, canals, and marshes. _____
4. They eat turtles, fish, muskrats, birds, and snakes. _____
5. Alligators have not one but three eyelids. _____
6. These reptiles lie on the ground or burrow into the riverbank. _____
7. An alligator's snout is short and wide. _____
8. A crocodile's snout is long and pointed. _____
9. You might wonder if you are being chased by an alligator or by a crocodile. _____
10. If its mouth is closed, look and see if its teeth are showing or hidden. _____
11. Do not stop or slow down to do this. _____

PART TWO: THE SENTENCE   93

12. Birds, fish, turtles, and humans are all alike to these animals. _____

13. They are appetizers, entrees, or desserts. _____

14. Zoos and animal parks are the best places to see these reptiles. _____

15. Some people make shoes, purses, and belts from their hides. _____

16. Canada and the United States have laws against this. _____

> The words "alligator" and "crocodile" have interesting origins. Look in a comprehensive dictionary to find out where each of those words comes from.

> Writers use different kinds of sentences according to their purpose in writing and their audience. A series of short sentences tends to separate ideas. This could create suspense, or it could help to clarify a complicated idea. Long sentences tend to speed up the action because a lot of ideas come to the reader all at once. Read some passages from different kinds of writing: a novel, a newspaper or magazine, a textbook. Identify sentences of different lengths. Discuss why you think the writers used short or long sentences. What effect were they trying to achieve? Were they successful?

REVIEW: THE SENTENCE AND ITS PARTS

FIND SUBJECTS AND VERBS

Underline the verbs twice and the complete subject once in this exercise. Circle the simple subject. Watch for compound subjects and verbs. You do not have to identify any of the other predicate parts or completions in these sentences.

1. Wolves are social animals.
2. Timber wolves and Arctic wolves roam the wilds of Canada.
3. The animals live in family groups.
4. The leader and his mate control the rest of the pack.
5. The group protects the older and weaker members.
6. All members feed and defend the young.
7. Wolves hunt in packs.
8. Weak or injured animals make the easiest targets.
9. The hunters place themselves along the trail.
10. Wolves hunt in relays.

Identify direct objects, indirect objects, and subjective completions

Circle the direct objects, indirect objects, and subjective completions in these sentences. Write "DO" if it is a direct object. Write "IO" if it is an indirect object. Write "SC" if it is a subjective completion.

1. Bram Stoker wrote the novel *Dracula*. _____

2. The real Dracula was a prince. _____

3. His given name was Vlad. _____

4. People gave him the nickname *Dracul*, which means dragon. _____

5. As king, he was a terrorist. _____

6. He murdered and tortured thousands of people. _____

7. He recaptured many fortresses from the Turks. _____

8. The Turks killed him in 1474. _____

9. In the past, Romanians told their children, "Be good or Vlad will get you." _____

10. Stoker's novel, as well as movies and plays, keep the legend alive. _____

11. Vlad did not kill people and suck their blood. _____

12. Stoker used him for the frightening effect of his name. _____

13. A certain disease produces the effects of pointed teeth, excessive hair, extreme sensitivity to light, and the need for blood. _____

(If you're interested, the disease is named *porphyria*. You might like to look it up.)

The best review you can make is to look over some of your writing. Read the sentences you wrote. Those are real sentences, not ones made up for a workbook. Find the subjects, predicates, objects, and subjective completions. Another good review is to take some sentences from a novel or a textbook you are reading and find the sentence parts in them.

KINDS OF SENTENCES

Sentences can be used in several ways. We could use a sentence to:
- make a statement
- ask a question
- give an order or command
- show some strong emotion

To show these different uses, our language makes changes in normal sentence structure. We still use subjects and predicates, but we may change the order in which the words occur. We also use different punctuation marks to show the intent of the sentence.

Example: Notice the differences in word order and punctuation.

    Darth Vader is a villain. (statement)
    Is Darth Vader a villain? (question)
    Avenge the Empire. (command)
    Avenge the Empire! (exclamation)

If the sentence is a command, the subject is often omitted (it is understood to be there).

Identify the kinds of sentences

Use the clues of word order and structure to identify the kind of sentence. Add the correct punctuation to each sentence. Write "statement," "question," "command," or "exclamation" to show what kind of sentence each is.

1. Did you go to the concert last night   _____
2. There were bands from all across Canada   _____
3. What a great show   _____
4. Don't miss the next one   _____
5. How many speakers did they use   _____
6. The whole arena was rocking   _____
7. Nearly half the young people in town were there   _____
8. You should have seen the costumes   _____
9. The flashing lights and the loud music made us all excited   _____
10. We danced in the streets after the show   _____
11. Did somebody call the police   _____
12. Move along   _____

13. Dina had a party after the show   _____

14. Have you heard what happened   _____

15. You should have been there   _____

In some of these sentences, you and your classmates may choose different punctuation. One person might say it is a statement; that person would use a period at the end. Another person might say it is an excited statement and would use an exclamation mark. Both people may be correct as long as they understand what the purpose of their sentence is.

> In a statement or command, if we wish to show strong emotion, we use an exclamation mark. However, there is no way to show strong emotion in a question. Still, we often want to express an excited question, for example, "Did you see that?" In speaking, we would make a gesture, raise our voice, and probably open our eyes wider. In writing, we have only a question mark. Perhaps you can invent a punctuation mark that could be used to show an excited question.

SENTENCE FRAGMENTS

You know that a sentence is made up of a subject and a predicate. If one of these parts is missing, the sentence is incomplete. An incomplete sentence is called a **sentence fragment**.

In spoken language, sentence fragments are used often. Listen to a conversation and you will note many incomplete sentences. The people who are talking are not confused. They see each other, they know what the conversation is about, and they use gestures, facial expressions, and tone of voice to help make their words meaningful.
Example: This is a conversation. Notice the fragments.
   "Hi."
   "Ready?"
   "No."
   "Why not?"
   "Because."

In written language the situation is different. Your audience is not in front of you. The members do not know what you are writing about until they begin to read. They cannot hear your voice or see your face or your gestures. You cannot see them, so you do not know if they understand you or not.

Therefore, written language is more formal than spoken language. That simply means we must be more careful about the form of language. If we are going to make sense to our audience, our written words are the only means we have to do so.

Part Two: The Sentence

That is why written language has spaces between words, capital letters, and punctuation. It is also why sentence fragments very seldom appear in formal language. If we give our readers only part of an idea, they will not know what we mean.

Recognize sentence fragments

For each group of words that is a sentence, write "S." For each group of words that is a fragment, write "F." If the words are a fragment, write "subject" or "predicate" to identify which part of the sentence is missing.

1. Is a lovely island in the West Indies _____
2. It consists of one main island and over a thousand smaller ones. _____
3. Most people _____
4. Towering mountains and rolling hills cover part of the island. _____
5. Has a magnificent coastline _____
6. Many tourists enjoy the sandy beaches and the coral reefs. _____
7. The capital city _____
8. For about 400 years, Spain _____
9. Has a population of about 11 million _____
10. The island is now ruled by a dictator named Fidel Castro. _____

Can you identify the island? The sentences and fragments above made the island a mystery to the readers. Don't let your writing contain mysteries that you don't intend.

Correct the sentence fragments

Add whatever words are necessary to make the sentence complete. Write the complete sentence.

1. Are a pair of lenses held in place in front of the nose by a frame

   _____

2. Wear them to correct faulty vision.

   _____

3. Increased when reading became more popular

   _____

4. Sunglasses and safety glasses
   _____

5. Focus light rays correctly
   _____

6. Must focus on the retina
   _____

7. If the rays do not focus, a blurred image
   _____

8. Harmful rays from the sun
   _____

9. Bifocals and trifocals
   _____

10. Contact lenses
    _____

REVIEW: USING COMPLETE SENTENCES

Identify sentences, sentence fragments, and run-on sentences

Write "S" if the group of words is a sentence. Write "F" if it is a fragment and then write "subject" or "predicate" to tell which part of the sentence is missing. Write "R" if it is a run-on sentence, and then draw a line between the two sentences that have been run together.

1. Tips for getting a job _____
2. Fill out the application form carefully. _____
3. An applicant should read over the entire form. _____
4. Some eager job seekers _____
5. Tell the truth when you are applying. _____
6. One way to lose a job _____
7. You should arrive at the interview on time. _____
8. Ate his lunch during the interview _____

PART TWO: THE SENTENCE

9. A young man took out his cell phone he called his wife. _____

10. The well-dressed, polite young person _____

11. An applicant became angry he threatened the interviewer. _____

12. The place of employment and its product or service _____

13. Never wanted to work there anyway _____

14. Think of possible questions. _____

15. Smile _____

16. Argue with the interviewer. _____

17. One applicant said he had a bomb in his briefcase he was going to blow up the office. _____

18. High school students with skills _____

19. Earn some money for her college education. _____

20. A person learned about the business the interviewer was impressed. _____

21. One fellow brought his dog to the interview it was not house-trained. _____

22. Everyone is a little bit nervous. _____

23. No one will hire me I have no experience. _____

24. I have no experience no one will hire me. _____

25. Coaching for interviews and applications _____

COMPOUND CONSTRUCTIONS

You have learned that any part of a sentence can be made up of more than one part. These are called **compounds**. We could have a compound subject, a compound verb, a compound object, or a compound subjective completion. If there are two parts to the compound, the parts are joined by "and," "but," or "or." If there are more than two parts, the first parts are linked by commas and a joining word is used before the last word in the compound.

A pronoun may be used with a noun as part of a compound, or two or more nouns or two or more pronouns could be used to make up the whole compound. Examples:
> *Beth* and *he* wrote the script. (compound subject made up of a noun and a pronoun)
> Jonathan helped *Lasa* and *him* with the costumes. (compound object made up of a noun and a pronoun)
> The applause was meant for *you* and *me*. (compound object of a preposition made up of two pronouns)

Compound parts can be confusing. In the subject of a sentence, it is correct to say "Melissa and I…." But sometimes we get into that habit when the compound is used as an object. When the compound is an object, the correct form is "Melissa and me…" To choose the correct form of a pronoun, use each part of the compound by itself with the verb.
Example:
> Mrs. Charles gave the free pass to Melissa and me. (Use "Melissa" with the verb "gave"; then use the pronoun with the verb "gave." You will see that "me," not "I," is the correct form.)
> The principal called Franca and me to the office. (The principal *called Franca*; the principal called *me*.)

Use the correct pronoun

Circle the correct pronoun. Describe how it is used (as subject, object, subjective completion, or possessive).

1. This small gift is from Franca and (I, me). _____

2. Danny and (she, her) discussed the choice. _____

3. The store clerk gave (he, him) and Dina a stony glare. _____

4. Our second buyers were Natalie and (she, her). _____

5. The card is addressed to Donato and (she, her). _____

6. Sami and (I, me) wrapped the gift. _____

7. Last year's social committee was Ted and (he, him). _____

8. Mr. Singh passed Craig and (he, him). _____

9. (She, Her) mother opened the door. _____

10. Franca's mother offered Danny and (I, me) a soft drink. _____

11. Let Maureen and (he, him) visit next time. _____

12. Roberto and (she, her) are also on the committee. _____

13. We told Franca and (they, them) the bad news. _____

14. The committee's advisors are (he, him) and Mrs. Vecchia. _____

15. (They, Them) and the parents donated money. _____

16. A speeding car almost ran into Felicia and (I, me). _____

17. The poem was written by Arturo and (she, her). _____

18. The guest instructors were Elvis Stojko and (he, him). _____

19. (He, Him) missed a great class. _____

20. The teacher scolded Chris and (she, her). _____

COMPOUND SUBJECTS AND VERB AGREEMENTS

Earlier we saw that some prepositional phrases appear to make the verb plural, but you should be careful to keep the singular with these.

The coach, *along with* the players, is in the gym.
The equipment, *as well as* the uniforms, is new.

To avoid this usage, use a compound subject.

The coach and the players are in the gym.
The equipment and the uniforms are new.

We studied compound subjects on page 92. A **compound subject** is made up of two or more subjects used with the same verb. A compound subject used with "and" is plural, as in the examples above.

A compound subject, used with "or" or "nor," is singular because we are talking about one thing or the other.

Either Rory *or* Nat is the president.
Neither Janice *nor* Wanda voted for them.

When one part of the compound is singular and the other part is plural, the verb agrees with the part closest to the verb.

Either the dancers or *Rena is* on next.
Either Rena or the *dancers are* on next.

USE THE CORRECT VERB WITH A COMPOUND SUBJECT

Circle the correct form of the verb in each sentence.

1. Neither Jeff nor his sisters (like, likes) cabbage.
2. His uncle and his mother (agrees, agree).
3. Either lettuce or peas (is, are) better.
4. The veggies and the argument (spoil, spoils) many meals.
5. Neither his father nor his friends (was, were) on his side.
6. Neither his friends nor his mother (was, were) listening.
7. Neither the complaint nor the reasons (sound, sounds) convincing.
8. Either Jeff or his sisters (start, starts) the trouble.
9. The main course and the dessert (is, are) delicious.
10. Neither sports nor music (interest, interests) us.
11. Candles and flowers (add, adds) a touch of elegance to the table.
12. Either Italy or France (produce, produces) that china.
13. Cake and candies (is, are) served later.
14. Neither the decor nor the lighting (appeal, appeals) to me.
15. Either the Kaplans or Tracy (make, makes) the dessert.

PART TWO: THE SENTENCE

16. The meat and the trimmings (taste, tastes) delicious.
17. (Is, Are) the dining room and the lobby full?
18. Either the waiters or the manager (order, orders) the food.
19. Neither the meal nor the surroundings (was, were) satisfactory.
20. The date and the problems (disappoint, disappoints) us.

SIMPLE SENTENCES

Before we go on to longer, more complicated sentences, let us review some basic facts about sentences.
- A sentence is made up of two basic parts: the subject and the predicate.
- The subject contains a noun or pronoun and its modifiers and tells what the sentence is about.
- The predicate contains a verb and its modifiers and perhaps an object or subjective completion.
- The predicate tells something about the subject.

The simple predicate is the verb. The simple subject is the subject of that verb.

The Leafs	lost.
(simple subject)	(simple predicate)
The Oiler fans	cheered wildly for their team.
(simple subject is "fans")	(simple predicate is "cheered")

Each part of the sentence may be compound; that is, a subject, verb, object, or subjective completion may have more than one part.

Compound Subject:	The centre and a defenceman scored.
Compound Verb:	The goaltender dove and caught the puck.
Compound Object:	The captain scored a goal and an assist.
Compound Subjective Completion:	The game was exciting and fun.

The sentences we have studied so far all express one main idea. They contain one simple subject and one simple predicate. These are called **simple sentences**.

Analyze simple sentences

Draw a vertical line between the subject and the predicate. Then circle the simple subject and underline the simple predicate.

1. Everyone has a name.
2. Your name may be your most precious possession.
3. All names have meanings.
4. Some family names come from a person's work.
5. Carpenter, Bishop, and Smith refer to occupations.

6. The names Hill, French, and Fleming refer to places.
7. Names such as Harrison, Mickelson, and Morrison come from the father's name.
8. People sometimes change their names in a new country.
9. The history of any name is important to know.
10. Many books can tell you the history of your name.
11. Many of the books refer only to English names.
12. Family names often have a long history.
13. Nicknames are names given to people partly as a joke.
14. A tall person might be called Sky or Shorty.
15. Writers sometimes choose a made-up name.
16. Some names have become words in our language.

> Research the history of your name. Your parents and other family members may be able to tell you a great deal about your family name and its history. Find out why you were given the names you have. Names are a good topic for expository writing.

COMPOUND SENTENCES

Simple sentences can be joined in the same way as the parts of compound subjects or compound verbs are joined. Use the conjunctions "and," "but," and "or" when linking sentences. These words are called **coordinating conjunctions** because they join (coordinate) the parts. Sometimes the parts of a compound sentence are joined by a semicolon (;). The ideas in the sentences being joined must have some related meaning, or the compound sentence will not make sense.

A compound sentence is made up of two or more simple sentences.
   The end of the term is near. Everyone is looking forward to a vacation.
   The end of the term is near, and everyone is looking forward to a vacation.
   You can stay here. You can leave.
   You can stay here, or you can leave.
   James went to Jamaica. His sister went to Trinidad.
   James went to Jamaica, but his sister went to Trinidad.
   Prices have been rising steadily. Experts think the rise will continue.
   Prices have been rising steadily; experts think the rise will continue.

Compound sentences are very common. They add interest and variety to writing and make sentences flow.

Analyze compound sentences

Circle the coordinating conjunction (or semicolon) in each sentence. Write the simple subject and the simple predicate in each part of the compound sentence.

1. Newspapers present the news, and journalists comment on events.

2. Newspapers shape public opinion, but some people say this can be harmful.

3. Editors must choose which articles to report, and they must leave some out.

4. Bias can affect their choices, or advertisers can try to control the content.

5. News events are the most common articles, but newspapers carry other features as well.

6. Columnists give advice of many kinds, and artists draw comic strips.

7. Fashion articles are very popular, but some of the fashions are expensive.

8. We can find movie listings in a paper, or we could find ads for vacation spots.

9. Publishing a newspaper is a big task; many different skills are involved.

10. Reporters and photographers are well known, but editors and machine operators are also important. _____

11. The newspaper must be delivered promptly, or all the work will be wasted. _____

12. Radio and television may report events sooner, but newspapers can give more depth to a story. _____

13. Canada has about 120 daily newspapers, and there are over 1000 weeklies. _____

14. You might think newspapers are a modern invention, but newspapers were in use in ancient Rome. _____

15. The Chinese invented the printing process, and they began publishing newspapers in the eighth century. _____

16. The Internet now provides access to newspapers all over the world, but many people want news of their own community. _____

17. Small communities publish their own newspapers, or they join to publish a county paper. _____

18. Newspapers can be a powerful source for good, or they can be used for harmful purposes. _____

19. The problem of bias is always present, and some newspapers are used only for propaganda. _____

Find out about your local newspaper. What careers are possible in the newspaper business? Many journalists start their careers by writing for their high school newspaper. If your high school does not have a newspaper, you might like to see if you and your friends could start one.

PUNCTUATING COMPOUND SENTENCES

The parts of a compound sentence are separated in one of two ways. One way is to use a comma before the coordinating conjunction. If you look back at the sentences in the last exercise, you will see many examples. The second way is to use a semicolon instead of the comma and the conjunction.

The use of a coordinating conjunction shows how the parts of the compound sentence are related.
- The conjunction "and" adds one idea to another.
- The conjunction "or" shows a choice between the ideas.
- The conjunction "but" shows a contrast between the ideas.
- The use of a semicolon does not show any particular kind of relationship, so it may not express your ideas in the way that you intend.

Sometimes an adverb is used with a semicolon to show more meaning. The adverb is then called a **conjunctive adverb** because it is being used to join the parts. The most common conjunctive adverbs are "however," "moreover," "therefore," "consequently," and "otherwise." A comma is used after the adverb. The sequence is semicolon, conjunctive adverb, comma.

Lightning struck the house; however, it did little damage.

Commas are being used less often than they once were. Sometimes the use of a comma is the writer's choice. Commas are often omitted in short compound sentences.

Jay won but I lost.   I'll wash and you dry.

If you think a comma will help your reader understand, then use it. If you think it is not necessary, leave it out.

Punctuate compound sentences

Place a comma or a semicolon wherever one is needed in these sentences. If a sentence does not need either, write "none." Be prepared to give reasons for your decisions.

1. Television can bring the world into our homes and our lives can be enriched. _____

2. News events are one kind of program but entertainment is the most popular kind. _____

3. About 98 percent of homes has a television set many have more than one. _____

4. The word form "tele-" means "far" and the form "vision" means "to see." _____

5. The first part of the word is from the Greek language however the second part is from Latin. _____

6. Television was first developed in the 1920s but it became important in the 1950s. _____

7. Television affects our lives in many ways therefore there are regulations about its use. _____

8. At one time, every home had an ugly antenna on its roof but now cable serves most urban centres. _____

9. Television channels are becoming more specialized consequently the number of viewers is divided. _____

10. Many different skills are needed to put a television show on the air and the industry employs thousands of workers. _____

11. Hundreds of performers appear on the screen but many more work on the show behind the scenes. _____

12. Programs were once broadcast live therefore every mistake a performer made was seen by all the viewers. _____

13. Most programs are taped now but some shows are still done live. _____

14. Television has had deep effects on politics and programs have changed how young people see the world. _____

15. Television is seen by some people as harmful however others say it can be used for great benefit. _____

> There are many interesting topics to research about television. Are you interested in how TV works? Would you like to have a career in television? Would you like to work behind the scenes or in front of the camera? What are some uses of television that have nothing to do with entertainment?

THE SUBORDINATE CLAUSE

A **clause** is a group of words containing a subject and its predicate. That should sound familiar because it is also our description of a sentence. We use the word "sentence" to describe the group of words standing alone. We use the word "clause" to describe each part when one sentence is combined with another.

In the last two exercises, we worked on combining two simple sentences into a compound sentence.

Megan is writing a story and Cal is writing a poem.

We have two simple sentences joined by the coordinating conjunction "and." We now describe the entire sentence as a **compound sentence**. A compound sentence is made up of two or more sentences joined by a coordinating conjunction. Each part of the sentence is now described as a clause. The structure is:

clause, coordinating conjunction, clause

There are three common coordinating conjunctions: "and," "but," "or."

In a compound sentence, the ideas in the two sentences are simply added to each other (and), stated as a choice (or), or contrasted (but). The clauses in the sentence are independent of each other. Each clause in a compound sentence is called an **independent clause**.

Often we combine sentences in such a way that one sentence actually becomes part of another.

The dog barks. It is alone.
The dog barks whenever it is alone.

The second sentence has become an adverb modifying the verb "barks," telling when the action occurs. The sentences have been joined by the conjunction "whenever." Because the second sentence is now part of the first one, it is called a **subordinate clause**. "Subordinate" means "less important."

Modifiers are less important in the meaning of a sentence than the words they modify. This clause is less important than the sentence of which it is now a part. Look at these examples.

> The crowd cheered loudly. (The adverb "loudly" is less important than the verb "cheered.")
> The crowd cheered for ten minutes. (The adverb phrase "for ten minutes" is less important than the verb "cheered.")
> The crowd cheered until everyone was hoarse. (The adverb clause "until everyone was hoarse" is less important than the verb "cheered" which it modifies.)

To summarize, an independent clause is a simple sentence that is joined to another simple sentence by one of the coordinating conjunctions (and, but, or). A subordinate clause is a simple sentence that has become part of another sentence as a modifier or as some other part of it. A subordinate clause begins with a **subordinating conjunction**.

Here are some common subordinating conjunctions. You will see that you already use these words in your writing.

after	because	so that	when
although	before	than	whenever
as	if	though	where
as if	in order that	till	wherever
as long as	provided	unless	while
as though	since	until	

Notice that many of these words relate to time and place. That is a clue that they often tell where or when an event occurred and begin adverb clauses.

Here are some different kinds of subordinating conjunctions.

how	that	why
what, whatever	which	
who, whom, whose	whoever, whomever	

Notice that several of these look like pronouns (who, whoever) and others look like noun markers (which, that). That is a clue that these are often used to begin noun clauses or adjective clauses.

Identify subordinate clauses

Underline the subordinate clause in each sentence. Circle the subordinating conjunction in the clause.

1. The band played while the people entered the auditorium.
2. The conductor, who was a senior, turned and smiled at us.
3. The percussion section played as if it was the only section.
4. The woodwinds, which were all played by first-year students, suffered badly from stuck reeds.
5. The leader simply smiled whenever a squeaking sound blared out.
6. The crowd talked loudly as though it wanted to drown out the noise.

Use subordinate clauses

Use a subordinating conjunction from the list above to change these simple sentences into subordinate clauses. Then add words of your own and write a complete sentence containing the subordinate clause.

Example: She works.   While she works, her sister studies.

1. Tad sprained his wrist.

    _____
    _____

2. Heather hears a noise.

    _____
    _____

3. We arrived.

    _____
    _____

4. Jan is moving.

    _____
    _____

5. The train is late.

    _____
    _____

Test your understanding by identifying what kind of subordinate clause you have written in each sentence.

THE COMPLEX SENTENCE

A **complex sentence** is a sentence that contains a main clause and one or more subordinate clauses. The sentences you worked with on the last page were all complex sentences. The sentences that you created in the second exercise were also complex sentences.

Main clause	Subordinate clause
We'll go	whenever you are ready
A dictionary is the reference	that I used
Sue asked the waitress	if she could have some water

Identify subordinate clauses

Underline the subordinate clause in each of these sentences. Circle the subordinating conjunction. Write "S" over the simple subject and "V" over the simple predicate of the subordinate clause.

1. If it rains, the party will be inside.

2. We planned for rain before we made the arrangements.

3. If Donald remembers, he will bring the decorations.

4. Mrs. Gonzales told us where the cutlery is kept.

5. After Joel had seen the menu, he decided he would come.

6. The crowd grew quiet when the lights dimmed.

7. Although the music was good, it was not loud enough.

8. No one could adjust the volume unless he or she had a permit.

9. The music always seems to be a problem when you have a big crowd.

10. I waited while the manager fumbled with the controls.

11. Natalia will not come to another party until she is sure of the music.

12. Krista understands more about the speakers than Armen does.

13. Has anyone heard from Kevin since he left?

PART TWO: THE SENTENCE

14. You should get plenty of complaints because people blame the organizers.

15. Ray brings a CD player wherever he goes.

16. Cynthia can't go to any parties for a month because she is grounded.

17. We can come here again as long as we book well in advance.

18. The music and the speaker system should be set up before the crowd arrives.

NOUN CLAUSES

You know that a sentence may have these major parts: subject, modifiers, verb, indirect object, direct object, subjective completion. A clause could be used as any one of these parts except the verb. In every case, the clause will be a subordinate clause.

We studied how nouns are used in sentences—as subjects, as indirect objects, as direct objects, as objects of prepositions, or as subjective completions. A noun clause is used in exactly the same ways. A **noun clause** is a subordinate clause that is used as a noun.

Many noun clauses begin with "that" or "what." Others may begin with one of these words: "whatever," "who," "whoever," "whomever," "where," "when," "how," or "why."
Example: Whatever you want to eat will be served.
            When I will be finished is still unknown.
            Why you like that song is something I don't understand.

IDENTIFY NOUN CLAUSES

Circle the noun clause in each sentence. State how each is used (subject, indirect object, direct object, or subjective completion).

1. I forgot what the teacher said.   _____

2. What the test will cover is a mystery to me.   _____

3. How I'll study for it is a problem.   _____

4. Everyone agreed that the test was coming.   _____

5. No one knew what would be covered.   _____

6. Alex doesn't know what he should do. _____

7. Whatever we study will be of some value. _____

8. The study centre provides help to whoever asks for it. _____

9. Luke's problem is how he will find time to study. _____

10. Michelle organized what everyone should work on. _____

11. What the class wants is more advance notice. _____

12. The class president has decided that she will make a complaint. _____

13. The vice-principal said that she would look into the matter. _____

14. Thomas knew where the meeting would be held. _____

15. A binder and all my notes are what I brought. _____

16. Whoever wants to help is welcome to attend. _____

17. Guillermo asked when the session would start. _____

18. The plan was that we would study together. _____

19. The teacher was amazed by how we performed on the test. _____

20. Parents were told why the students had done so well. _____

ADVERB CLAUSES

A complex sentence contains one or more subordinate clauses. One kind of clause found in a complex sentence is the adverb clause. An **adverb clause** is a subordinate clause used as an adverb. An adverb clause can modify a verb, an adjective, or another adverb. Adverb clauses often tell *how, when, where, why,* or *to what extent.*

After he had written his answer, Ted read it over carefully.
He lost several marks *because he made foolish mistakes.*

Identify adverb clauses

Underline the adverb clause in each of these sentences. Circle the subordinating conjunction. Write "S" over the simple subject and "V" over the simple predicate of each adverb clause.

1. When the first Olympic Games were held, a foot race was the only event.

2. Track and field was almost unknown until it became popular in the nineteenth century.

3. Although foot races were common, races on measured tracks were not.

4. When the first modern Olympic Games were held in 1896, track and field was included.

5. Women's events were not part of the Olympics until the Games were held in 1922.

6. As track-and-field events became popular, many famous athletes set new records.

7. Paavo Nurmi of Finland became famous when he broke world records 35 times.

8. Babe Didrickson made women's sports popular at the 1936 Olympics, where she won two gold medals.

9. Many events have changed since they were first introduced.

10. Although the records set during the 1950s seemed unbeatable, few of them remain.

11. Because training methods are better, athletes are stronger and faster today.

12. Donovan Bailey became famous when he won an Olympic gold medal in 1996.

13. Athletes need the best of medical care when they are training.

14. Serious injuries can result if a strict program is not followed.

15. Track events are more popular because they receive wide media coverage.

Create adverb clauses

Join the two simple sentences by making one of them into an adverb clause. Use the conjunction in parentheses as the joining word. The first sentence is done as an example.

> The Olympic Games are going on. Millions of people watch on television. (while)
> While the Olympic Games are going on, millions of people watch on television.

1. Sponsors now compete for broadcast rights. The Games can be used for selling their products. (because)

2. Canadian athletes make us proud. They perform so well at the Olympics. (when)

3. Facilities throughout Canada give young men and women places. They can train all year. (where)

4. Many young athletes want to qualify for the Olympics. They are able to. (when)

The Olympic Games have become a major event of worldwide interest. There are many aspects of the Olympics besides the events themselves. You might like to research and write about some of the non-sports features of the Olympics. How are the Olympics planned? How is the site chosen? Have the Games ever been held in your province or city? The Games have become closely linked with politics. How has this affected the Olympic Games? Or you could research some of the great athletes who have taken part in the Games. Or you could write about a role that you would like to play at the Olympics, either as an athlete or in some other way.

ADJECTIVE CLAUSES

An **adjective clause** is a subordinate clause used as an adjective. Adjectives modify nouns or pronouns, or are used as subjective completions. Adjective clauses are used for exactly the same purposes. They often answer the question *what kind?* or *which one?* when describing the noun or pronoun. Adjective clauses usually come after the word they modify.

This is the book *that I told you about.*
This is the house *where I used to live.*

The words "that," "which," "who," "whom," and "whose" are often used to start adjective clauses. They are called **relative pronouns** because they relate the clause and the word it modifies in a special way.

The student left the room.   The student came back.
The student *who* left the room came back.

The relative pronoun "who" replaces the determiner and noun "the student" when the simple sentence is made into a subordinate clause. Relative pronouns act as both pronoun and conjunction.

The relative pronouns "who," "whom," and "whose" replace nouns or pronouns that refer to humans.
The relative pronoun "which" replaces a noun or pronoun that refers to something non-human.
The relative pronoun "that" replaces a noun or pronoun that may refer to either human or non-human.

To summarize, relative pronouns have three functions:
1) They introduce adjective clauses (as conjunctions).
2) They replace a noun or pronoun in the sentence being changed into a clause (as pronouns).
3) They act as subject, object, or subjective completion in the subordinate clause that is formed (as noun or pronoun).

Manitoba was the fifth province that joined Confederation. ("That" is the subject of "joined" in the adjective clause that modifies the noun "province.")

The woman with whom I worked is now the manager. ("Whom" is the object of the preposition "with" in the adjective clause that modifies the noun "woman.")

Identify adjective clauses

Underline the adjective clause in each sentence. Circle the relative pronoun and mark "S" over the subject of the clause and "V" over the verb.

1. The theatre is a career that attracts many people.

2. The actors who are so skilful are exciting to watch.

3. There are many schools in Canada that prepare young people for the theatre.

4. On-stage performers are the people that we see most often.

5. There are many other artists and workers who are vital to a performance.

6. The stagehands who work backstage prepare the sets and scenery.

7. The costumers design the clothing that must be perfect.

8. The playwright who provides the story and words is very important.

9. The role of the director, which includes responsibility for telling the story on stage, is perhaps the most important of all.

10. Many theatre people get their start in school plays and in amateur productions that are held in small local theatres.

CREATE ADJECTIVE CLAUSES

Combine the two simple sentences into a complex sentence. Make one of the simple sentences into an adjective clause. Use the relative pronoun in parentheses as the joining word. Write the complex sentence that you create. The first sentence is done as an example.

There are four kinds of stages. The stages are used in the theatre. (that)
There are four kinds of stages that are used in the theatre.

1. The proscenium stage is one kind. This kind is found in many schools. (that)

   _____

   _____

2. The open or thrust stage is often used in theatres. These theatres put on Shakespearean plays. (which)

   _____

   _____

3. Theatre in the round is another kind. The audience surrounds the actors on three sides. (in which)

_____

_____

4. The type of stage is a factor. The factor affects how the play is presented. (that)

_____

_____

5. Actors perform on any kind of stage. The actors must always remain in character. (who)

_____

_____

> Look over some of your recent writing. Find some adjective clauses that you have used. See if you have used relative pronouns correctly.

REVIEW: SUBORDINATE CLAUSES

The only way to identify a subordinate clause is to see how it is used in a sentence. If the clause is used as a noun, it is a noun clause. If the clause is used as an adjective, it is an adjective clause. If the clause is used as an adverb, it is an adverb clause.

Identify the subordinate clauses

Underline the subordinate clauses in the sentences below. Write whether each is a noun clause, an adjective clause, or an adverb clause.

1. When Arab troops marched into Damascus on Oct. 1, 1918, thousands of people cheered. _____

2. The cheers were partly for a young Englishman who rode with the troops. _____

3. The movie which was made about this man was titled *Lawrence of Arabia*. _____

4. The Arab leader had asked that the British support him in his war against the Turks. _____

5. The British sent T.E. Lawrence, who spoke Arabic, as an observer. _____

6. They knew that he had spent four years in Syria as an archaeologist. _____

7. As well as working as an archeologist, Lawrence had become a spy. _____

8. After ruling the Middle East for hundreds of years, the Ottoman Empire was falling apart. _____

9. England was one of several nations that wanted to take over this area. _____

10. When the British seized Egypt in 1882, they gained control of the Suez Canal. _____

11. Lawrence was bored by normal duty, which included making maps and writing reports. _____

12. As a way to gain the confidence of the Syrians, Lawrence adopted their lifestyle and clothing. _____

13. Lawrence became a master of guerrilla warfare, which was the most effective way to fight in the desert. _____

14. He was briefly held by the Turks, who probably did not know who he was. _____

15. Lawrence endured terrible torture, which he wrote about in his book. _____

16. The British army realized that Lawrence's rebel army was more successful than it was. _____

Create subordinate clauses

Join the simple sentences by making one of them into a subordinate clause. Use the conjunction in parentheses.

1. The Turks greatly outnumbered them. Lawrence's troops had them pinned down. (although)

   _____

2. The war ended. The Syrians were disappointed with the results. (when)

   _____

3. The British had signed a secret agreement with France. The British still controlled much of the area. (who)

_____

4. Lawrence was bitter and ashamed. He learned of the result of his work for the Arabs. (when)

_____

VARIETY IN SENTENCE BEGINNINGS

The usual order of English sentences is
> subject, verb, object (or indirect object, or subjective completion)

Writers often vary the beginnings of sentences to add interest for the reader. If you start with a part that is not the subject, you hold the subject in suspense from your reader. If you start with a verb, you can add impact and emphasis with the action word. If you start with a modifier, you draw attention to that idea.

Four ways to vary sentence beginnings:
1) Put an adverb before the subject.
   Softly, Jane hummed a tune as she studied.
2) Put the verb before the subject.
   Away *went* all her plans for the weekend.
3) Begin the sentence with a prepositional phrase, a participial phrase, or an infinitive phrase.
   For us, the choice was clear.
   Choosing her words carefully, she explained the problem.
   To make sure, she checked the date on her calendar.
4) Begin the sentence with a subordinate clause.
   As she explained her predicament, the others began to understand.

> Reread each sample sentence, placing the subject first. What different effects do you find in the meaning or impact of the sentences?

VARY THE SENTENCE BEGINNINGS

Rewrite each sentence below. Change the position of words to give variety.

1. The dog followed us, wagging its tail.
   _____

2. We tried to send it away by waving our arms.
   _____

3. The dog followed us all the way into the school.
   _____

4. The whole thing seemed like a big joke to Raymond.
   _____

5. The vice-principal arrived, looking quite severe.
   _____

6. We explained what had happened as best we could.
   _____

7. Our goal was to be sure that we were not in trouble.
   _____

8. Several students nearby were listening in.
   _____

9. The dog finally left with a forlorn look in its eyes.
   _____

10. It was still at the front door two hours later.
    _____

You should not change the beginning of a sentence just for variety. You should change the sentence so that it has more impact on the reader. Then you are writing effectively.

> It is not incorrect to have the subject first in every sentence, but it is not good style. Good writers are not only correct, they also have style. Check over some of your recent writing. See if there are sentences that you could improve upon by starting them differently.

COMPOUND–COMPLEX SENTENCES

You have learned that a compound sentence is made up of two or more simple sentences joined by a coordinating conjunction (and, but, or) or a semicolon.

You also know that a complex sentence is made up of a simple sentence (the independent clause) and one or more subordinate clauses. The subordinate clause is part of the independent clause, acting as a noun or a modifier.

A **compound–complex sentence** is both of those types put together. A compound–complex sentence is made up of a compound sentence in which one or all of the independent clauses contain one or more subordinate clauses.

Compound sentence	independent clause (and, but, or) independent clause
Complex sentence	independent clause containing a subordinate clause
Compound–complex sentence	independent clause containing a subordinate clause (and, but, or) independent clause

Independent Clause	Subordinate clause	Independent clause
Gina knew	that she would be late	but she didn't care
Carl was surprised	when he was chosen;	he didn't expect it

Analyze compound–complex sentences

Underline each independent clause and circle each subordinate clause. State what kind of clause each subordinate clause is (noun, adverb, adjective).

1. Manuel knew who the thief was, but he would not tell us. _____

2. After we entered the room, we began to talk casually, and he stayed outside. _____

3. When we were all in the room, a hysterical laugh was heard from upstairs, and we all ran to the bottom of the stairs. _____

4. Manuel was standing at the top of the stairs, where he sneered down at us, and he was holding a small key. _____

5. Greg said that we should go upstairs, but we were too nervous to start. _____

6. The people that Manuel had invited were present, but we still had no clues. _____

7. We had done what Manuel requested, and now we were waiting for him to speak. _____

8. Manuel simply smiled, which was making us more nervous, and then he started down the stairs. _____

9. The rest of us were so confused that we just stood there, and Manuel walked right past us. _____

10. Somehow he had found out who the thief was, but we did not know how. _____

11. We followed Manuel into the living room where we stood silently; we were completely puzzled. _____

12. Melissa, who is Joel's friend, reads a lot of detective stories, but she was also confused. _____

13. Theft is a serious crime that is punishable by imprisonment, and a thief might steal again. _____

14. Since Manuel was still silent, we began to ask him questions; he merely smiled at us. _____

15. Manuel waited until we were quiet again, and then he began to explain the case. _____

> This is the beginning to what could be a good story. Finish the story by writing an exciting murder mystery.

PART TWO: THE SENTENCE

REVIEW: USING COMPOUND AND COMPLEX SENTENCES

REVIEW COMPOUND SENTENCES

Combine the two simple sentences into a compound sentence, using the conjunction in parentheses. In each clause, mark "S" over the subject and "V" over the verb. Use whatever other punctuation may be necessary when you combine the sentences.

1. The cone had a hole in the bottom. The ice cream was dripping out. (and)

2. The babysitter had paid for it. Now she had no money left. (but)

3. The child began to whimper. The sitter knew what would happen next. (;)

4. She could comfort the child. She could try to distract him. (or)

5. The ice cream was dripping on the child's shirt. The sitter now had a bigger problem. (and)

6. She was not supposed to buy him treats. She couldn't resist. (but)

REVIEW COMPLEX SENTENCES

Combine the two simple sentences into a complex sentence, using the conjunction in parentheses. In each clause, mark "S" over the subject and "V" over the verb. You may need to use pronouns to make the sentences correct.

1. A boomerang is a flat, curved instrument. A boomerang is used as a weapon or for sport. (that)

2. A boomerang spins. It is thrown correctly. (when)

3. Some are shaped. They return to the thrower. (so that)

4. Boomerangs are used by Australian Aborigines. Aborigines use boomerangs for hunting. (who)

   _____

5. Boomerangs strike an object with more force. A rock would have less force. (than)

   _____

6. Aborigines sometimes decorate boomerangs. Aborigines use boomerangs in ceremonies. (which)

   _____

7. The Frisbee flies in a similar way to a boomerang. Some people think the Frisbee was inspired by it. (because)

   _____

8. A skilful player throws a Frisbee. A Frisbee may curve, hover, or travel in a straight line. (when)

   _____

9. Frisbee golf is played by thousands of people. Frisbee golf requires skill and precision. (which)

   _____

A REVIEW OF SENTENCES

For each sentence, write "simple," "compound," "complex," or "compound–complex" to tell what kind it is. Circle the simple subject and the simple verb for each clause.

1. In the Old West, barbers often performed minor surgery. _____

2. Dentists had some knowledge of medicine and they were often forced to do a doctor's work. _____

3. Operations, which were done without anaesthetic, were extremely painful. _____

4. Wounds that were inflicted in battle often resulted in amputation. _____

5. Much less was known about medicine in those days, and thousands of people who died during the American Civil War might have been saved if they had received better care. _____

> Select a few sentences from your writing that are examples of the kinds we have studied. Exchange your sentences with a classmate and identify the kinds of sentences as we have done in this exercise.

THE LAST WORD

If you have worked your way through most or all of this book, you deserve a break. The sentences below illustrate grammar rules by breaking them. Read each sentence and discuss what rule or guideline it is supposed to illustrate. We hope you find the exercise amusing.

1. Each pronoun agrees with their antecedent.
2. Just between you and I, subject and object forms of pronouns differ.
3. Verbs has to agree with their subjects.
4. Watch out for irregular verbs which have creeped into our language.
5. Don't use no double negatives.
6. A writer musn't shift your point of view.
7. Join clauses good, like a conjunction should.
8. Don't write a run-on sentence you got to punctuate it.
9. About sentence fragments.
10. In letters themes reports articles and stuff like that we use commas to keep a string of items apart.
11. Don't use commas, that aren't necessary.
12. Its important to use apostrophe's right.
13. Don't abbrev.
14. Check to see if you any words out.

If you are one of those people who start a book at the end, study the rest of this book to figure out what is going on here.